The Salsa Culture
Invades America

FÉLIX VALENZUELA

Copyright © 2017 Félix Valenzuela
All rights reserved
First Edition

PAGE PUBLISHING, INC.
New York, NY

First originally published by Page Publishing, Inc. 2017

ISBN 978-1-68348-838-5 (Paperback)
ISBN 978-1-68348-839-2 (Digital)

Printed in the United States of America

Contents

Preface 9
Acknowledgments 11
The Plight of the Immigrant..16
Life in the Barrio 23
The Barrio Dwellings...26
    Personal Hygiene...30
    Tragedy Strikes the Family 31
    Coping with Poverty 31
    Common Infestations..33
    The Infamous Neighborhood Toilets 34
    Laundry Washing and Neighborhood Feuds......34
    Typical Mexican Food 36
    Homemade Tortillas 36
    Hot Atole 37
    The Jaguar Club 37
    A Boiling Hot Starch Accident 38
Los Braceros 40
El Paso as a Tourist Attraction 45
The Impoverished Slum Area Known as Chihuahuita....48
Corporal Punishment in the School System..................49
A Man Named Aoy 51
Academic Discriminatory Measures
    against Immigrants (1920–1926) 58
The Arrival of Television and its Impact
    on Entertainment in El Paso...................................62
The Gangs of South El Paso and the Pachuco 65
Pachuco Slang from the Barrio 68
"Vamos al Chuco"—Let's Go to El Paso 81
Mexican American Acculturation into Mainstream
    United States—Its Dilemmas and Implications 84

Taxonomy of Cultural Terms 87
    Spanish People 87
    Hispanics 87
    Latino 88
    Mexican 88
    Mexican American 88
    Hispano 91
    Chicano 92
How to Put an End Forever to All Discrimination 93
The Barrio Witch Doctors
    —"Los Curanderos" 96
The Medicinal Application of Indian Herbs 103
The Consequential Marriage of the Indian
    and the Spaniard Gives Birth to the Mexican 108
The Socio-Culture of Love and Power in the Mexican Family 113
The Mexican Macho Man 118
El Rey 121
Storytelling in the Barrio 123
    La Llorona 124
    The Magic Stones 128
    The Two Compadres 131
    The Little Match Girl 139
Sayings from Our Grandparents 143
Chiquillados 145
Mexican Riddles—"Adivinanzas" 147
The Songs of the Mexican Revolution 150
St. Valentine's Day Celebration 153
Honoring the Dead 155
Las Posadas—Reenacting Joseph and Mary's Journey 157
Two Mexicans Visit Jerusalem 158
Cinco de Mayo Celebration 159
The Sixteenth of September Celebration 161
Halloween 163
Matachines 166
Quinceañeras 168
Mexican Mariachis 172

Mexican Piñatas 175
The Origins of Mexico and Its Builders 181
The Latino around the World...187
Leaders Who Have Impacted the Mexican Mind and Spirit 189
    Benito Juarez...189
    Jose Vasconcelos 189
    Dr. Diana Natalicio 190
    Dr. Hector P. García 190
    César Chávez...191
    Corky Gonzalez...191
    Sonya Sotomayor 192
    Raymond Tellez..192
    Danny Olivas 193
    Dennis J. Bixler-Márquez, Ph.D...193
Classic Mexican Songs..195
Classic Favorite Mexican Recipes...200
Bibliography and Recommended Reading...................................217
Sources..223

To my wife Esther and our three children, Linda, Felix, and Lizette.

Preface

Much has been written about the Mexican experience in the United States of America, and there is a need now to define "Mexican" as the designation is now in a category with many other names: Chicano, Latino, Hispanic, and Mexican American. Since I grew up in the barrio (settlement) of South El Paso, I probably fit into all of these categories, a discussion topic included in this book. Several serious topics are discussed, but overall, this book is a celebration of the arrival in the United States of the Mexican and how we have influenced the American lifestyle.

Most of us know Mexican culture goes back centuries into the heart of the magnificent pyramid structures from the Mayan and Aztec civilizations, but we may not have given thought to how great the impact of these ancient engineering and mathematical skills has been, and that the Mexican culture was established long before the Spanish conquistadors. Although I find this part of history fascinating, *The Salsa Culture Invades America* basically covers the time period beginning with the early 1900s through the first ten or so years of the twenty-first century.

In the early 1900s, the immigrants from Mexico, who crossed the border into the United States of America, brought their religion, ancestral beliefs, and all of their customs. For the most part, they were seeking a better life and made many sacrifices along the journey. Hopefully, through this writing, the Mexican immigrant's wealth of history will bridge some very important gaps of misunderstanding with the American society and, perhaps, the world at large. The Mexican's close-knit communal existence has been the subject of much study by familial researchers in particular. With its own lifestyle and with its ancient roots, the Mexican immigration contributes an unparalleled, colorful cultural experience.

FÉLIX VALENZUELA

    I also hope that through my pen, many descendent of Mexican immigrants will discover the God-given purpose that awaits them as they prepare for the new and heavy tasks ahead along the path of the American Dream.

Félix Valenzuela

Acknowledgments

Foremost, I appreciate the Mexican immigrant legacy which has inspired the making of this work. As readers ponder the historical events of the Mexican experience, they should open themselves up to their own inquiring minds and promptings so that this book can hopefully enrich their understanding of an important and outstanding people from south of the border.

I am thankful for the love and support of my wife Esther and our children Linda, Felix, and Lizette, who have contributed immensely to the motivation behind this book. Many of the messages of this book are really directed at them and also at their children largely to expand their insights into their own cultural background. Esther has been my source of inspiration and delight in dealing with life's challenges in a meaningful and productive manner. I owe much to her for believing in me despite my shortcomings in life. She has been the kindness and most generous person I have ever met and loved. Her examples of dedication, leadership, unwavering patience, endurance, and commitment to the goodness in this world are virtues I admire by far and faithfully struggle to be worthy of in our marital relationship. I will always respect her highly for putting up with me. Her understanding and appreciation of my own abilities, talents, and gifts has inspired the overall work behind this book.

I am deeply indebted to Dr. Berta Martinez, whose masterful and professional literary artistry led to the undertaking of translating this work from English into the vibrant Spanish language which required the preservation of the Spanish language's cultural sensitivity and its unique, colorful romanticism. Dr. Martinez was instrumental in providing assistance in vital aspects of this book and exerted herself over and beyond the call of duty, so to speak, in the implementation of ideas culminating from her own expertise of Mexican history.

I also appreciate the moral support from my loving sisters, Dolores Sierra, Natalie Cervantez, and Mary French. I value their continued concern for my life and family. They are part of, to a great extent, the people directly and indirectly depicted in the contents of the book.

Dr. Blake and Carol Wayman have been remarkably true and faithful friends. Their love and understanding will forever be treasured and deeply imbedded in my own psyche. It was Carol who greatly encouraged me to write this historical record. True friends like them come only once in a lifetime. I cherish their hospitality, leadership abilities, sincere thoughtfulness, faithfulness, virtue, firm beliefs, steadfastness, and all their contributions to the making of this world a better place to live in. I admire them deeply.

My friend Jaime Castro has been a pillar of strength and fortitude in the midst of my own obstacles in life and an abundant source of unwavering wisdom and intelligence for my sake to seek after. He is, above all, a righteous friend I can count on to bring out from our own psyches the innermost feelings. The many exchanges of ideas between us over the last forty-five years are something I treasure wholeheartedly.

Bishop Moroni Flores and his wife Margarita introduced me to a higher plateau in the understanding of life and death and the need for constant nourishment of thought, plus the establishment of good actions in my daily existence. They have provided meaningful help and demonstrated unrestrained kindness, love, sincere concern, and leadership when I have been in dire need of all these elements in my lifetime. I am thankful to them for inspiring my mind and gently softening my heart throughout our association of more than fifty years. I will forever cherish their friendship, their intellectual pursuits, and their dedication in defense of cultural dignity and respect.

I am hopeful that my grandchildren Eden, Bella Rose, Robert Anthony, Briana, Ryan, Lauren, Keira, Hailey, Ethan, Cozette, Ada, Kayden, Alayna and Colin James will be encouraged to read the contents of this book in the future.

Dr. Joseph L. Allen has been instrumental in guiding me into inquiry of the complexities involving research and study. His prominence in the field of archeological investigation and writing has led me to perform my own curious undertaking to sincerely understand Meso-American civilizations. He has inspired me as a mentor to my psyche in all areas of life. I will always be grateful for Dr. Allen's clear perceptions of history, which has awakened in me the desire to continue in pursuit of truth and wisdom. His wife Rhoda has been extremely kind and generous and a wonderful example of virtue and faithfulness to me and my family. I owe much to his love and appreciation of my humble talents. He is a mighty, wonderful, and diligent leader of men.

Manuel and Hilda Gonzalez are among the most influential people that have crossed paths with mine. Together, we have maintained a long-lasting relationship of trust and friendship. They are intellectually endowed with the spirit of investigation also and are culturally-refined individuals who have accomplished much in the way of knowledge, familial closeness, and cultural understanding. I am thankful to them for inspiring much of this historical writing.

Dave Mojica has been a trusted friend who has unselfishly shared much with me along the road of integrity, leadership, honesty, and success in regards to the "American Dream." His keen understanding of humanity is ever present in his daily life as he continues to serve people in general. His involvement as governor of the sixty North Texas Optimist Clubs is outstanding. Having received the Silver Beaver Award from the Boy Scouts of America Dave Mojica has only added to his Prominent role as a prized leader. His valor during the Vietnam War is matchless coupled with his administrative abilities over the Department of Veterans Affairs, Vietnam War, in El Paso and in Waco, Texas. That amounts to a complex but worthy life of an individual with above reproach character and allegiance to a noble life. Dave will certainly be inducted into history as an exceptional American due to his intellectual and professional stature. His family will be the beneficiary for generations to come of a genuine love and kindness that is rare and powerful in our society at-large. Hispanics, Latinos, and Mexican-Americans alike will bless his name forever. Thanks, Dave, for everything. Dave and I have counseled together about a multitude of issues surrounding our religious beliefs and have enjoyed archeological exchanging of data associated with Meso-American. Your humorous way of establishing good and positive attitudes among your fellow men is deeply instilled in my own psyche. I will always recall your thought on the wall of your cabin that says, "A man's castle is his home until the queen arrives."

Shirley Bass has been an inspiring intellectually endowed friend whose profound abilities dealt with the educational arena, writing addresses, and general governmental speeches that have built up political leaders for many years. Presidents and governors alike have contracted Shirley's natural talent in script writing. Shirley has been an overwhelmingly kind and generous presence in my life, and I owe her much for those noble qualities. Her pursuit of happiness is readily felt as one embraces her inner qualities of industry, motivation for self-improvement solely linked to consistent hard work, vision, dedication, and engagement in sound and worthwhile endeavors. I will always be grateful for having met Shirley Bass.

In the end, I have learned more than I could ever write in these pages. I also know that in the next few years I will have learned much more and thus will probably want to add and change parts of this book (this is the risk and reward of serious study). Nevertheless, read on and let us share this learning experience together as one mind and thought. Numerous people who have insisted that it might very well serve as a historical record and an educational instrument of sorts to inspire youth and adults alike motivated this compilation.

Ellis Island European Immigrants

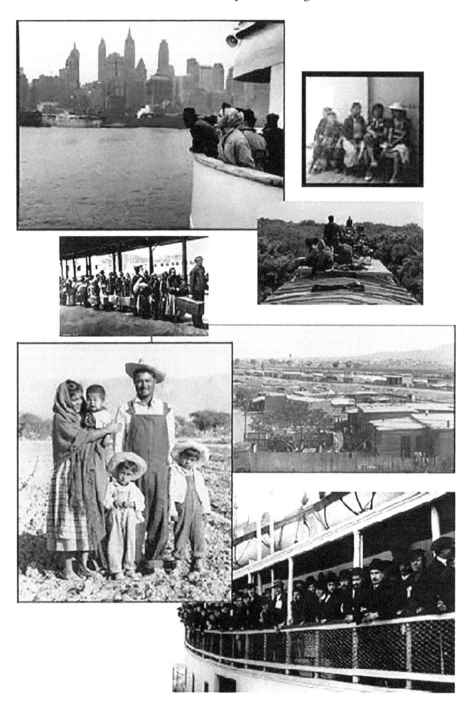

Mexican Immigrants entering the U.S.

The Plight of the Immigrant

Immigrants from other nations are closely linked to the experience of the Mexican immigrants who faced similar difficulties in their quest to secure life away from, in many instances, the treacherous system of their former countries. Most of the time, the European nationals, like the Mexican immigrants, hoped to find a new and everlasting place of opportunity. However, upon their arrival in the United States, they first had to deal with the harsh realities of economic uncertainty and a generally unkind reception. Guadalupe Valdés in her book, *Con Respeto*, has done an excellent job describing the experience of immigration:

> Hundreds of thousands of immigrants have entered this country since the beginning of this century (1900). For people who were born in this country, however, it is often difficult to imagine what it was like for early immigrants to leave their countries and to arrive in the United States. The reopening of Ellis Island in 1990, however, brought to life for the American people the moment of arrival in the United States of many of these individuals. Using old pictures and moving recollections of a number of now fully established former immigrants, the media sought to paint a picture of the determination, hopes, and dreams of those who arrived in New York, saw the Statue of Liberty, and prayed that they would be allowed to remain in this land of opportunity. For these Ellis Island immigrants, the process of coming to the United States during the early part this century (1900) involved a decision to leave the home country, a long and often difficult journey,

and a definite moment of arrival and entry into the United States. What is clear from the Ellis Island Museum archives is that for these early immigrants, there was a precise moment in which the home country was left behind, and a precise moment in which they entered the United States. Many documents of the period offer evidence of the fact that many of these individuals could later recall the exact dates of these events, their feelings at the moment of departure or arrival, and even the detailed circumstances of the processing routine. In many ways, arrival and processing at Ellis Island had the effect of a legal ceremony or ritual that forever after changed the lives of these "new" Americans.

In contrast to the Ellis Island experience… there was no legal ceremony and no ritual at the moment of arrival (for the Mexican immigrant). For these largely borderlands people, their coming across to live in the United States (rather than to buy goods or work temporarily) was not the result of a long and difficult journey. Most had spent time in the United States on numerous occasions, and most had relatives here.

For the women and children, the move from the villages to the border [U.S./Mexico] was the first step in bringing the family together after years of absence and periodic visits. Once on the border, the experience of having crossed or having attempted to cross the border legally or illegally became a familiar one. In some cases the illegality was low-risk and simply involved borrowing someone else's border crossing card or green card in order to go shopping in El Paso for several hours. In other cases it involved walking across the river at night or early morning and spending weeks or months working as domestic servants in El Paso homes. It was even the case that a few of the women spent periods of several months with their husbands who were already in the United States, leaving their children behind with relatives in Juarez. These long stays usually took place in anticipation of a permanent move and often involved looking for housing, examining available options.

The experience for the men was somewhat more traumatic. For most of them, crossing into the United States involved leaving their towns in rural Mexico when they were in their late teens or early twenties and entering the United States illegally. Some men had connections and leads that helped them cross the river and relatives who helped to find them work. Others made it on their own, to the border area, to Juarez, and then across the shallow muddy waters. None of the men spent much time living or working on the Mexican side of the border. They crossed as soon as they could and persevered in crossing and re-crossing. For the most part, all the men (in the Valdés study) had spent years in the United States before they moved their families to Juarez.

Again, in contrast to Ellis Island immigrants, most of the Mexicanos (in the Valdés study) entered the country illegally or helped their families to do so. Whatever trauma was associated with coming across, then, had to do with the fear of getting caught and with the fear of having to go back. In every case, the illegal status of one or more family members made them feel vulnerable. For years at a time, they lived with the knowledge that at any moment they or members of their family, including their children, could be arrested by the border patrol and sent back to Mexico. The fact of being illegal made them easy targets for exploitation and for blackmail by angry neighbors and even resentful relatives.

Hordes of Mexican nationals fled from their devastated lands and the economic turmoil resulting from the Mexican Revolution of 1910, arriving in the United States of America under circumstances similar to the people who touched down at Ellis Island, New York. They were penniless and destitute, hoping for a brighter future on the other side of the great river of the north, the Rio Grande.

Mario T. García in his book, *Desert Immigrants*, describes the entry into El Paso, Texas:

> The new arrivals were the forebears of today's Mexican Americans and Chicanos...Besides being the largest port of entry (El Paso), this border site between 1880 and 1920, the years of its greatest economic growth, supplied jobs for large numbers of unemployed Mexican workers as it surged from an obscure desert town to an "instant City." As El Paso and the Southwest contributed to the new industrial state, Mexican immigrants augmented its swelling multi-racial working class.
>
> The booming southwestern economy, largely extractive and agricultural, provided immigrants with mainly menial work. Needing only a minimum of skilled personnel, the railroads, mines, smelters, and farms expanded and prospered because of their use of unskilled Mexicans....In El Paso the relationship between the economy and the condition of Mexican immigrants is visible. Based on the region's underdevelopment limiting job advancements for workers, a class society functioned with distinct

racial divisions. Mexicans were primarily blue-collar workers whereas Americans were mostly white-collar employees, businessmen, managers, and professionals. Such a system produced profits and privileges for the city's employers while restricting wages for all workers—both Mexicans and Americans—although nonetheless dividing them along racial lines. The small and weak local American Federation of Labor, for example, consistently fought against the employment of alien labor in El Paso and directed its animosity and frustration more at Mexican workers than at American bosses. This interaction among class, race, and labor in El Paso involved occupational distribution, wage standards, and the relationship of organized labor to the Mexican working class.

Education might have helped to close the economic gap between Mexicans and Americans but so-called Mexican schools in the barrios only contributed to the disparity.

During one of those historic crossings into the United States of America, my grandparents came across from Mexico and arrived in Clint, Texas, where they settled during the Mexican Revolution. They eventually moved westward to South El Paso, referred to then as El Chuco (slang for El Paso) or El Segundo Barrio (the second ward/settlement), where I was born on October 11, 1942, to Felix Ochoa and Maria Inez Carreon at Thomason General Hospital.

The familial address in the barrio was 713 Tornillo Street, located at the tip of the railroad crossing at Cotton Street and perpendicular to the original Bowie High School. I was named Felix Ochoa III. I was the sixth and youngest of the siblings in the Ochoa family.

After suffering considerable economic hardship in South El Paso, my family eventually found permanent employment with the railway system. Texas and Pacific (T&P) and Southern Pacific (SP), recruiting unskilled laborers for its lines during the 1940s, hired the head of the Ochoa family, my mother Maria Inez Carreon Ochoa, who by then was a divorced mother of six. Later on, the eldest of her children, Domingo, was also employed by the Texas and Pacific. That opportunity was long sought by the Ochoas, and it rid them of poor working conditions and gave them a more stable economic circumstance, plus they acquired new, nontraditional skills. Both my mother, Maria Inez, and my brother Domingo remained permanently employed with T&P the rest of their lives.

Top: My grandmother Victoriana Zapata (seated) surrounded by her children. My father is standing on the right. Bottom (both): My grandparents on my mother's side Teresa and Jesus Carreon.

Life in the Barrio

The exact origins of the Ochoa and Carreon families are not clear. Some members claim their actual history commenced just before the Mexican Revolution in the region of Valle San Buena Ventura located in the state of Chihuahua, Mexico. They allege that somewhere in time, uncles Pepe, Santos, and Samuel (part of the Carreon clan) wore the armor of Pancho Villa before fleeing from him to escape the ravages of war and civil unrest in Mexico. They arrived in the United States of America in the early 1900s. They crossed the northern part of the Rio Grande and landed in Clint, Texas, where my mother was born. The real reason why these brothers fled from General Villa and why Villa's soldiers went after them, to no avail, is not clear. Was it because they too, like the stories of Villa's other soldiers, had accumulated wealth behind his back from the cities they ransacked during the Villistas revolutionary exploitations? Sufficient to say, most Villistas lost everything due to philandering, drinking, gambling, and sexual rendezvous with women.

Sometime after, that part of the Carreon clan, which had settled in Clint moved westward to south El Paso (El Segundo Barrio) where my mother Maria Inez Carreon married Felix Ochoa. They had six children: Alicia, Domingo, Dolores, Maria, Natalia, and me, Felix. Fred Morales in his book, *El Segundo Barrio*, writes:

> The Segundo Barrio is geographically located in South El Paso and has always been a poor Mexican quarter of El Paso. Its primary boundaries have been El Paso Street to the west, Paisano to the north, Cotton to the east and the Rio Grande River to the South. [Back] in 1887, the City of El Paso was divided into four "wards" or political districts when R.C. Light body was mayor of El

Paso. The Second Ward was called the Segundo Barrio by the Mexican-Americans who live there.

In the early 1800s many cottonwoods or "alamos" grew in this area resembling a small forest which the people called the "bosque." A road called the "Camino Nacional" or the National Road ran through the area, from Ponce de Leon's rancho (today's downtown El Paso) to Paso Del Norte (Ciudad Juarez). This road, also called the Public Road, cut through the bosque and connected with a street in the ward or "partido Chamizal" in Juarez called Lerdo Street. At this time near the end of present-day Park Street in El Paso, was a ford to cross the river called "Vado Irigoyen."

In 1834, Santiago Alvarado became the first known settler of the Segundo Barrio. He was granted a small plot of land to farm and soon became a "campesino" or farm worker. Around this time the Governor of Chihuahua was Jose Joaquín Calvo and the local prefect of Paso Del Norte was Alejandro Ramirez. The Alvarado farm was watered by the "acequia del Chamizal" which ran about two blocks to the south.

In 1852, a land grant was awarded to James Manning by the Republic of Texas, located in the northeast portion of South El Paso where today is called the Alamito section. Manning had participated in the Battle of San Jacinto during the War of Independence from Mexico.

When Anson Mills platted his map in 1859, the primitive streets in South El Paso were El Paso, Oregon, Utah, Stanton and Kansas.

The area, known as the bosque or thicket, was used by the Apaches to help them raid Paso Del Norte in bold, daring daylight attacks. These raids were primarily to steal livestock. A watchtower was built close to the Mission of Guadalupe to warn residents when the Indians were attacking. Later, as settlers moved northward, the bosque was cleared and mud houses called "jacales" were built. The cottonwoods provided timber and as a result of the clearing, the Apaches lost concealment from which to launch their attacks. As the land was cleared it was leveled and obstructions removed for agriculture and irrigation. These new arrivals brought their Mexican culture, customs, beliefs and societal patterns with them. They built many adobe homes and small acequias. The first settlers to arrive in the area were the Avocatto, Barragan, Lama, Alderete, Peinado, Valencia and Escajeda families.

The Segundo Barrio by 1950 (This would be eight years after I was born.) was a horrible slum area of close to 50,000 people living in less than a square mile and had one of the highest infant death rates due to diarrhea in the nation.

The Barrio Dwellings

Conditions in South El Paso or El Segundo Barrio were not like those found in the fashionable circles of society at that time. People in the barrio settlement or presidio lived in substandard dwellings that were only a step up from the mud houses or jacales abounding in Chihuahuita, the area south of present downtown El Paso. These one-story apartments with approximately 400–500 square feet of living space were built at the turn of the century. They typically contained one bedroom, a small living room, a kitchen with a two-burner stove, an ice box (refrigerator), and a table big enough to seat two people. A local ice company delivered blocks of ice twice a week to keep the refrigerator cool and keep the food from spoiling. The lone bedroom contained a bed that could accommodate three to four people and an unattached/portable closet. The living room was fitted to accommodate a sofa, a table lamp, and a sofa chair. The dwelling had no heating or cooling and had no insulation in the walls or ceiling. There were no inside toilets, bathrooms, showers, nor running water.

In my family, the younger members took turns hauling water in pails ("baldes") or jars ("jarros") from an outside faucet. This faucet was used for general purposes by the entire neighborhood ("vecindad"). At one point in time, we were six children living together along with our great grandmother Victoriana Zapata, our parents, and Tia (Aunt) Concha. The living room was used as a bedroom at night. The family enjoyed listening to a record player which played size 78 records and later the smaller size 45. The 45s were eventually replaced decades later by the introduction of Super 8 track tapes. Then the Super 8 tapes became obsolete when the smaller cassette tape was introduced into the market.

The barrio. We lived in 713 Tornillo and Cotton Street.

Don Toma's grocery at the corner.

My mom, Soledad Valenzuela. The little boy in the plaid shirt is my cousin, Lorenzo Reyes. I'm the one in front with the tie and suspenders.

My cousins all dressed up. Felix Ochoa III.

Maria Inez Ochoa, the one who gave birth to me, in the T&P Railroad Yard.

Most of the apartments were brick construction. Two wood frame doors were in the front as entry to the kitchen while the other served as the northeast entrance of the structure, plus there was one window that was on the east side and the other one on the north side of the apartment. The kitchen enclosure was made of what appeared to be half-inch thick wood siding on the wall and exposed 2 x 4 materials of the interior.

Due to the lack of insulation and the lack of a heating or a cooling system, winters were cold and harsh and the summers were unbearably hot and sweaty inside the dwelling. A portable kerosene burner ("calentón de petroleo") was the only source of heat to keep the family warm during the winter. The fumes and foul smell from the kerosene often caused breathing problems. The odor was strong and noxious. The fumes caused headaches and uncomfortable sleepless nights for the family members. The kerosene was also used to light the "luces o lámparas de bombílla" (overhead lights or lamps) at night.

Since the family was not able to afford motorized fans to cool the hot summer days, as kids, we preferred to spend most of our time playing outdoors under the shade of the cottonwoods, Chinese elms, and the more common nonbearing mulberry trees, or wherever we could find protection from the hot El Paso sun. Adults would also take advantage of the shaded cottonwoods when they came home from work or whenever they were free from their jobs. They routinely sat in the "sillas" (chairs) to chat with others, sometimes until the late hours of the night. The women folk separated themselves from the men to talk about the latest rumors or other events in the daily neighborhood happenings. Men joked and poked fun at women talk. Their own chats were mainly centered around the Mexican Revolution and times past, bullfighting, some fishing tales, obscene jokes, working conditions at their place of employment, but mostly, down-to-earth things affecting them and their families in their new country. They entertained each other while drinking cerveza (beer) or "te" (tea), "orchata" (milk drink), or "agua de melón" (cantaloupe drink) during weekdays. The tequila Mexican-made liquor was reserved for weekends.

During the quiet of the evening, these conversations outside could be heard from different parts of the presidio. Consequently, everybody knew all the rumors, scandals, and notoriety surrounding the vecindad (neighborhood). Oftentimes, fights and quarrels would break out abruptly between people due to misunderstandings, disrespectful jokes, or personal things about each other or their families. These apparently occurred due to a great degree of overindulgence in tequila or too much cerveza.

Personal Hygiene

Saturdays called for children to take their weekly bath in the "tina," a circular aluminum tub, similar to the drinking basins used for cattle. Unfortunately, since I was the youngest of the six children in the family, I had to wait for my turn after the older kids.

By the time my turn came around, I had to bathe in the same water used consecutively by my older brother and my sisters which, by then, was full of "jabon del borrego" o "jabon de lejía" (lamb or lye soap.) And after repeated usage by all the older children, the water was dirty. That soapy, dirty water irritated my skin and caused severe dryness, and there was no cream. I earned the nickname of "manos de lagarto" (alligator hands). The infamous soap created cracks in my skin, giving my hands an unsightly and disgusting appearance. I was embarrassed, and I grew very self-conscious of my hands. I used to hide them from the children and others at school and the neighborhood people as well.

Besides being known for its dryness, the soap smelled terrible. There were times when the same lye soap was employed to punish kids for unruly behavior. Parents would make their children hold the soap inside their mouth until they could no longer stand the awful stench, similar to technique applied to "Ralphy from the famous Christmas Story movie" (1959-1961). The experience deriving from that form of punishment was a constant reminder to children to behave and obey at all times or else face the consequences. The soap had a horrible taste, and it was somewhat sickening. The smell in the mouth was long-lasting and at the punishment's end, it caused some to actually vomit and spit desperately onto the ground.

Tragedy Strikes the Family

My father Felix R. Ochoa was assaulted one night as he was leaving a check-cashing place, possibly a local cantina (drinking bar.) An unknown assailant(s) hit him with a blunt instrument and made a deep wound in his head. They stole all his weekly earnings and left him for dead. Tragically, air entered the open wound and caused damage to his brain. His reasoning was affected and he was unable to communicate normally for the rest of his life. There is very little information related to what transpired in my family after that incident, and also it is not known why my parents divorced thereafter. Unfortunately, my father was later sent to a sanatorium in the city of San Antonio, Texas where he spent sixteen years away from his children and died at the age of fifty-four years on June 7, 1957, at 7:45 p.m.

He had been a tall man, more than six feet in height but was rather slim. He was born on April 2, 1903, to Felix Ochoa and Victoriana Zapata. He was seven years of age when the Mexican Revolution started and he was in his teens when he rode with Gen. Pancho Villa.

Apparently he had worn tight-fitting shoes which caused an infection resulting in a "cancerous ulcer of his leg." His "antecedent morbid" condition underlying the cause of his death was "Septicemia." After the viewing at the Akers Funeral Home he was buried in the San Jose Burial Park cemetery in San Antonio. Frances Truax, his sister, refused to have his body sent to El Paso.

Coping with Poverty

My father's unfortunate disability left only my mother Maria Inez to care for and feed all six of us hungry kids. She worked for the T&P Railroad system and continued in that employment for the next several decades. Her meager pay, paid biweekly, was around 35 cents an hour, and the days were usually twelve to fourteen hours long. In the late 1940s and early 1950s, a large 16 oz. RC Cola cost three cents and two tacos were five cents.

Maria Inez's meager earnings were barely enough to pay the rent for the apartment, which was about $12 or $15 a month, but somehow, she managed to provide the basic essentials of food and clothing for her family. Unavoidably, she was continually borrowing money to help ends meet. After payday, the family would head across the border to Juarez, Mexico, and buy food as it was cheaper there. She spent the rest of the money on second-hand clothing: shoes, socks, underwear, and coats. When the times were plentiful, and those were rare, new clothing and other inexpensive items were bought to make up for bad times. Normally, shoes and the clothing had to be worn for an entire year. By year's end, the shoes had holes at the bottom and usually the sole had split loose and created a liplike opening in the front. The separated sole of the shoe caused an embarrassing flapping sound. During rainstorms, walking was really a problem. Water seeped through the bottom of the torn shoe and drenched the foot. Running with torn shoes was bothersome. Thank goodness for summertime when kids for the most part walked barefoot. By the beginning of the next school year, new clothing replaced the old. In spite of the lack of facilities to wash clothing, families were forced to wear the same clothes over and over without concern for general body odors or smelly feet.

When economic circumstances permit, the clothes, usually those worn by the older kids in the family, were sent to Deras cleaners. Deras picked up the clothes and then brought them back to the barrio. It was expensive, considering the condition of the economy during that time, but since all the barrio inhabitants were poor, there was no other standard for comparison, and no one seemed to know the difference. They dressed, ate, enjoyed similar activities outdoors, went to the same schools, and worshipped at the same church.

Entertainment at the "kermés" (carnival at the local St. Ignatius Catholic parish) was held once or twice a year. Hard-earned money was used to buy food and play games there. On one occasion, the Ringling Brothers Circus came to South El Paso and set up their huge tents at the Skidmore Field next to the old Bowie High School. Sixteen kids, including me, were selected to pile into a Volkswagen and be driven to the center of the circus arena. The gigantic spotlight focused on us, and everyone applauded as we struggled to climb out of the car. We were squashed up and had very little room to move or breathe but we got in free of charge! It is now baffling as to why Ringling Brothers decided to bring all their entertainment to the most impoverished section of El Paso, but regardless, we barrio kids got in free to the applause of clowns, aerial artists, and other circus personnel. There were also trained horses and some caged wild animals inside the big tent.

Common Infestations

Lice ("liendres") infested most of the neighborhood kids. Sleeping in crowded conditions helped speed the infestation of these unwelcome pests. Also, unsanitary conditions and mingling with other barrio children who were known carriers had its obstacles. Although proper medication was a welcome relief to help keep us from scratching our heads all the time, it was scarce and not always available. Lice were uncomfortable and a nuisance to most kids in the barrio. That malady had no end and it did not discriminate.

Another problem people had to fight off was the "chinchis" (bed bugs), perhaps the most aggravating of all. The chinchis caused us to sleep miserably at night because of their unpredictable bites. Different kinds of foul-smelling disinfectant chemicals were routinely spread over the mattresses but to no avail. It seemed as if these tiny creatures were hidden everywhere, and it was almost impossible to get rid of them.

Barbers had crude disinfectants they applied as preventative measures against fungicide, virucide, and other related maladies. They applied them lightly on young customers known to be carriers of hair bugs. Haircuts were a welcome relief. The lice disappeared for a time until the hair grew back.

School officials were careful not to get close to barrio kids because of their lice problems and, normally, kept their distance whenever they had to deal with them at school. The officials made matters worse by sending threatening letters to the parents about their children's infestations. Despite the seriousness of spreading the lice among the students, school officials did very little to help the students or their families. The beleaguered children were oftentimes seen scratching incessantly in the schoolroom as well as in the playground during recess and physical exercise.

The Infamous Neighborhood Toilets

There were no indoor bathrooms in the apartments. One had to go outside and go to the back of the apartments where the toilet rooms were located. Once entered, a ghastly scene unfolded, especially at nighttime. The crudely brick-constructed rooms were infested with rats, mice, roaches, annoying flies, pesky mosquitoes, and other insects. Conditions inside the toilets were undesirable, unsafe, and uncomfortable. Newspaper material was used in place of soft tissue paper because it was less expensive to purchase. Usually, the newspaper was too thick to flush down, so it was thrown on the floor. Since there were no lights inside the toilet rooms, people burned the newspapers for light, especially during the night. Devoid of ventilation, both the hot and cold weather made these toilets unhealthy. Also, they were narrow on the sides, a tight squeeze, and had high ceilings. Water was filtered down a thick metal pipe leading from a ceramic-like holding tank at the top of the room. The newspapers clogged up the toilets on a daily basis and filthy water regularly ran over the top of the toilet bowl onto the floor. There was, of course, always a foul odor. The situation was completely unsanitary, but the presidio people had no alternative.

Laundry Washing and Neighborhood Feuds

Most people performed their daily washing outside. A couple of concrete pads with water faucets and measuring approximately 3 x 3 feet in diameter were available for washing clothes. Sometimes barrio people used these pads out in the open to wash their own bodies and their children. These ground-based washing areas were large enough to accommodate two women at the same time doing their laundry side by side. This laundry area was the center of neighborhood gossip and talk in general. The conversations kept the women abreast of all happenings in the presidio. For the most part, laundry washing created amicable relationships, but once in a while, things would get out of hand. Presidio womenfolk would verbally fight for space, and that would lead to unpleasant arguments. Everybody would get involved while others would come outside to witness the airing of ill feelings and badmouthing. Others just peered from their windows to get a glance of the whole scenario.

Feuds between people were commonplace elsewhere in the presidio. The matriarch of the Ochoa family, my mother, Maria Inez, was routinely involved in a number of feuds against the Carreon, a one-legged uncle whose name was Jose or Pepe. He lost a leg as a result of falling off a train; his leg was amputated. For unknown reasons in the past, my mother hated El Tio (uncle) Pepe. She went out into the middle of the neighborhood "pasillo" (pathway) and openly cursed El Tio Pepe, who, incidentally, was often only a few feet away peering out from his apartment window. Tio Pepe never came outside to confront her. Instead, he defended himself by yelling obscenities from inside his apartment. It was quite a lively entertainment for all the spectators who often witnessed this charade inside the vecindad (settlement).

Although the battles were loud and disgraceful, they rarely led to actual physical harm. El Tio Pepe and Maria Inez were complete opposites of each other. She was an imposing, tall woman and twice as heavy as he was. It was estimated at one time that she measured five feet nine or ten inches and weighed over two hundred and fifty pounds while El Tio Pepe weighed around one hundred and forty pounds and his height was close to five feet six inches. They never made any positive efforts at friendship during their mortal lives, and they implored the families to bury them away from each other upon death. It is not easy to understand the extreme hatred they both had for each other. Remarkably, they were cousins, came from similar backgrounds, and underwent almost the same hardship in Mexico and in the barrio of South El Paso.

The feuds and the exchanges of profanity in the presidio exposed neighborhood kids to obscene language at an early age. Almost every bad word was well-known by the kids in the barrio. Feuds were commonplace, and in some cases, they developed into violent disturbances and the police had to intervene.

Typical Mexican Food

The most exciting part of the month was market day and everyone looked forward to it every other Saturday. The market place was located across the border in Juarez where bargains could be made. Food was cheaper to purchase in Mexico, but the travel was difficult and tiring. One had to carry different kinds of bags full of "el mandado" (groceries) in the "trambillas" (electric street cars.) It was a welcome sight when the small refrigerator and the cupboards were full of goodies. That meant eating "patas de marrano en vinaigre" (pig's feet bottled in vinegar), "frijóles de la olla" (beans from the pot), soft flour tortillas, chile jalapeño (green chili), "arroz españól" (Spanish rice), "queso" (cheese), "leche" (milk), "pan de dulce" (sweet bread), "vegetales" (vegetables), "papas" (potatoes), "maíz" (corn), freshly made "caldo de rés" (soup with a mixture of vegetables, potatoes, carrots, and boiled spare ribs), "chiles rellenos," tacos, enchiladas, tostadas, tamales, burritos, gorditas, flautas (rolled tacos), and the making of menudo (boiled cow hide, pig's feet, and hominy.) The food had to be rationed so that it would last for two weeks until the next payday and extra care had to be taken so the food didn't spoil.

Homemade Tortillas

Flour tortilla making was the life of the presidios (neighborhoods.) There was an endless supply of freshly made tortillas in all households, which could be spread with butter and a dash of salt added for greater taste. Tortillas were part of every meal. Three to five dozen tortillas would normally take almost a half day for people to make, but in a matter of minutes, they were gone. Each member of the family would sometimes consume three of four tortillas without stopping. It was an effective way to calm hunger in between meals. The tortillas were used for all general eating purposes in the family. This food is nourishing despite the high cholesterol that was unknown to people at the time and indispensable as the Ochoa's and Carreon's daily food supplement.

Hot Atole

Atole was a gruel made by boiling Indian corn that had been pounded to flour in water and also in milk. It was especially made during wintertime to keep one warm. This drink not only quenched one's thirst, but it also provided families with a form of dietary supplement. In the country of Peru, it is called "mazamorra."

The Jaguar Club

Becoming a part of and participating in the activities of a club was an entry into another reality of the barrio. We were known as the Jaguars. As part of our initiation, we were required by the leaders of the Jaguar Club to tattoo our arms and legs. On our arms we tattooed our complete names, and on our left leg, we engraved the tattoo of a cross with five lines to represent rays from the sun. These were symbols of our new allegiance and the comradeship in the club. The tattoos had a very penetrating effect upon our psyches. They made us feel tough and gave us the illusion that we looked mean. Actually, the tattoos were really designed to instill loyalty within the ranks of the club.

One of the gravest acts of the Jaguar Club took place on an unforgettable night when the members broke into railroad cars and stole food items. Boxes of strawberries from the Texas and Pacific Railway (T&P) were stolen and carried away by six members of the club.

Railroad security officers ran after them armed with rifles and pistols. The shots from their weapons missed the running youths. The watchmen were eluded and left far behind. The cover of night had provided protection from those officers who were determined to kill the thieves. Safely arriving back at our homes, we made sure the strawberries were well hidden away. Wishful thinking.

The day after this serious episode, the goods were discovered in their secret places, and the perpetrators of the crime were revealed. In my case, news of the stolen strawberries came to the attention of my older brother Domingo, an employee of T&P. He immediately conducted a deep interrogation of the Jaguar Club members and discovered that his own little brother was one of the culprits. He found the strawberry boxes hidden in a closet covered with my clothing. He yelled and screamed at me until he realized the situation would cause problems with his own employment, so he took no action. He did, however, remain very upset and used threats to keep me in line and gave me many activities associated with his daily responsibilities and/or chores in the house. And in a quiet celebration away from the neighborhood, he and my sisters ate all the strawberries without me.

Soon after that episode, I decided to quit my membership in the Jaguar Club, concluding that it was not in my best interest to continue the activities with my peers, such as beer drinking barrages, cigarette smoking, and potential criminal acts. Later on, a dramatic scholastic change took place—I went from having a previous low performance in school to above-average grades in my classes. I spent more productive time in wholesome ventures away from bad influences in the barrio through earnest activity in the realm of religion.

A Boiling Hot Starch Accident

Natalia (Tala), my older sister by one year, and I were fighting over a lollipop next to the washtub, which was full of boiling hot starch, one summer morning. As we struggled to try and pull the lollipop away from each other's hands, I slipped and fell into the hot starch, which had been prepared for the family's clothes.

Starch was customarily used to prevent wrinkles on clothes and make them appear stiff, similar to the stiffness of military uniforms. When I felt the hot starch, I cried out loud in excruciating pain while my sister tried desperately to pull me out of the tub. What seemed like an eternity inside the boiling starch actually only lasted a matter of seconds, but it was long enough to cause severe burns all over my legs. Unable to stand the tremendous pain, I ran hysterically outside into the street in just my underwear, yelling madly. My cousins and some older kids saw me running wildly and chased after me. It required the best runners from among them to finally subdue me and carry me back to the apartment where my mother tried hopelessly to calm me down and ease the pain. She applied her own homemade remedies to the skin that was now full of blisters. But it was in vain, and they rushed me straight to a doctor's office downtown where I almost passed out.

The doctor applied painkilling medications over my legs and punctured the dozens of blisters with a sharp needlelike instrument. Each time he popped open a blister, I screamed. It was the first time I had ever experienced burns on any part of my body. I just could not contain myself. It was painful. After several hours in the doctor's office, I was taken home. In the ensuing days, high fever engulfed me, and I spent some sleepless nights. The healing process lasted several weeks. As a result of this grievous altercation, my legs became thinner because of the loss of so much skin tissue on both legs.

Los Braceros

The Bracero program ("bracero" means manual laborer, one who works using his arms) was a series of laws and diplomatic agreements initiated by an August 1942 exchange of diplomatic notes between the United States and Mexico for the importation of temporary contract laborers from Mexico to the United States.

We know about the real experience, and this, like other programs, was misused, misunderstood, had its benefits and had its down side and tragedies. Here is an overview, and I suggest the reader research this subject on his or her own. It is the basis for much of the current controversy over the United States' immigration policies.

Even though the United States had made use of migrant Mexican labor in its agricultural sector since the early 20th century, such labor tended to be both migratory and seasonal, with many workers returning to Mexico in the winter. The situation changed with the involvement of the United States in World War II, which caused a massive labor shortage in all sectors of the economy with the transfer of much of the nation's active labor force into the various armed services. The extreme labor shortage forced the United States into changing its immigration policy, resulting in development of the bracero program in conjunction with Mexico.

The bracero program was a guest-worker program that ran between the years of 1942 and 1964. Over those 22 years, the Mexican Farm Labor Program, informally known as the "bracero program", sponsored some 4.5 million border crossings of guest workers from Mexico (some among these representing repeat visits by returned braceros). Many braceros succeeded in securing green cards and legal residency while others (known as "quits") simply left the fields and headed for work in the cities. As of 2014, millions of Mexican Americans trace their families' roots in the US to their fathers' or grandfathers' arrival as braceros.

Recent information suggests that the program generated controversy in Mexico from the outset. Mexican employers and local officials feared labor shortages, especially in the states of west-central Mexico that traditionally sent the majority of migrants north (Jalisco, Guanajuato, Michoacan, Zacatecas). The Catholic Church warned that emigration would break families apart and expose braceros to Protestant missionaries and to labor camps where drinking, gambling, and prostitution flourished. Others deplored the negative image that the braceros' departure produced for the Mexican nation. The political opposition even used the exodus of braceros as evidence of the failure of government policies, especially the agrarian reform program implemented by the post-revolutionary government in the 1930s. On the other hand, historians like Michael Snodgrass and Deborah Cohen demonstrate why the program proved popular among so many migrants, for whom seasonal work in the US offered great opportunities despite the poor conditions they often faced in the fields and housing camps. They saved money, purchased new tools or used trucks, and returned home with new outlooks and with a greater sense of dignity. Social scientists doing field work in rural Mexico at the time observed these positive economic and cultural effects of bracero migration. The bracero program looked different from the perspective of the participants rather than from the perspective of its many critics in the US and Mexico.

US businesses increasingly realized that provisions within the program ensured an increase of costs for the imported labor. The program mandated a certain level of wages, housing, food, and medical care for the workers (all payable by the employers) that kept the standard of living above what many had in Mexico. This not only enabled many to send funds home to their families but also had the unintended effect of encouraging illegal immigration after the filling of quotas for official workers in the US.

These new illegal workers could not be employed "above the table" as part of the program, leaving them vulnerable to exploitation. This resulted in the lowering of wages and not receiving the benefits that the Mexican government had negotiated to insure their legal workers' well-being under the Bracero program. This, in turn, had the effect of eroding the US agricultural sector's support for the program's legal importation of workers from Mexico in favor of hiring illegal immigrants to reduce overhead costs. The advantages of hiring illegal workers included such workers' willingness to work for lower wages, without support, health coverage or in many cases legal means to address abuses by the employers for fear of deportation.

Nevertheless, conditions for the poor and unemployed in Mexico were such that illegal employment seemed attractive enough to motivate many to leave to work within the United States illegally, even if that directly competed with the legal workers within the bracero program leading to its discontinuation.

In 1956 the publication of the book, *Stranger in Our Fields*, by labor organizer Ernesto Galarza drew attention to the conditions experienced by braceros. The book begins with this statement from a worker: "In this camp, we have no names. We are called only by numbers." The book concluded that workers were lied to, cheated, and "shamefully neglected." The US Department of Labor officer in charge of the program, Lee G. Williams, described the program as a system of "legalized slavery."

Labor unions that tried to organize agricultural workers after World War II targeted the bracero program as a key impediment to improving the wages of domestic farm workers.[45] These unions included the National Farm Laborers Union (NFLU), later called the National Agricultural Workers Union (NAWU), headed by Ernesto Galarza, and the Agricultural Workers Organizing Committee (AWOC), AFL-CIO. During his tenure with the Community Service Organization, César Chávez received a grant from the AWOC to organize in Oxnard, California, which culminated in a protest of domestic U.S. agricultural workers of the US Department of Labor's administration of the program. [45] In January 1961, in an effort to publicize the effects of bracero labor on labor standards, the AWOC led a strike of lettuce workers at 18 farms in the Imperial Valley, an agricultural region on the California-Mexico border and a major destination for braceros.[46]

César Chávez

The end of the bracero program in 1964 was followed by the rise to prominence of the United Farm Workers and the subsequent transformation of American migrant labor under the leadership of César Chávez and Gilbert Padilla. Dolores Huerta was also a leader and early organizer of the United Farm Workers. According to Manuel García y Griego, a political scientist and author of The Importation of Mexican Contract Laborers to the United States 1942–1964, [47] the Contract-Labor Program "left an important legacy for the economies, migration patterns, and politics of the United States and Mexico." Griego's article discusses the bargaining position of both countries, arguing that the Mexican government lost all real bargaining-power after 1950. (*Wikipedia*)

El Paso as a Tourist Attraction

Mario T. García in his book, *Desert Immigrants*, writes:

> As a tourist attraction Ciudad Juarez also benefited certain American businessmen. Owing to the closing of El Paso's red light district and gambling houses by 1910, many American operators shifted their trade across the border and helped initiate Juarez's dependency on tourism from El Paso and the United States....Aware of Juarez's, as well as other Mexican border towns', uneven economic development in comparison to El Paso, the Revista Internacional of Juarez observed in 1917:
>
> "Our towns live in poverty, being wholly tributary to our neighbors. We have no industry, no agriculture, and lack a means of support. Other than what the local braceros [commuters] earn, in addition to the bull fights, the cock fights, the lotteries, liquor and curio shops which delight the tourists who visit us."
>
> Along with the climate, El Paso used its Mexican connection to entice tourists. It advertised that they could easily cross the border at El Paso and visit Ciudad Juarez and other locations in northern Mexico. Here they would find a new cultural experience. An 1890 travel description emphasized that strangers had to make a trip to Juarez. Everything in the old Mexican town would be of great attraction, including the houses, streets, the old church, and the system of irrigation. "The habits, customs,

and life of this primitive people are indescribable as a whole... but very interesting." A later chamber of commerce article entitled "El Otro Lado" (The Other Side) assured potential tourists that Ciudad Juarez was "typically Mexican."

To the visitor who approaches the Mexican border for the first time "the other side" is the chief point of attraction. Ciudad Juarez lies just across the river from El Paso, and is reached by a ten-minute drive or electric car ride. Juarez, with its 8,000 people, is typically Mexican. The old church-centuries old, one of the oldest on the continent-with its massive adobe walls; the amphitheater for bull-fighting, the plaza, the streets, the business houses and dwellings, the curio shops, the vehicles from the surrounding country, the personal appearance, dress, and customs of the people are all full of novelty and interest to the American visitor. Our Mexican neighbors are accustomed to being made the target of curious American eyes. The Mexican is nothing if not courteous, and the humblest peon will meet and converse with you with at a degree of manly dignity and courtesy that commands not merely respect but admiration.

In its international edition of 1903, the "Times" bluntly emphasized El Paso's interests... Mexico, the land of romance, of sunshine, of the Aztecs, the Moquis, the Yaquis, the home of the adobe, the serape, the reboso; the nativity of the chile, the enchilada and the frijole [sic]; Mexico, the El Dorado of Cortez, of Alvarado, of Acquila; the land of gold and silver and copper; is before us for study, for inspiration, for reflection and, perhaps, more than anything else for profit.

El Paso Electric Company, No. 1 Mule Car.

The Impoverished Slum Area Known as Chihuahuita

The Chihuahuita slums, known as "jacales," were a step lower than the apartment comforts of South El Paso. Dogs and cats often ran wild in the streets unvaccinated against rabies in addition to rats infesting the toilet compartments. In the early 1900s, the South El Paso scenario was not as horrid as the people who lived in Chihuahuita. Mario T. García writes:

> Huts and hovels where families of from three to eighteen were existing in a condition of squalor and misery indescribable.
>
> A family of eighteen persons consisting of the father, mother, their nine children, grandmother and father, and five relatives, was found huddled in a 'dobe' house just south of the canal in the rear of Santa Fe Street. All were seated round in the room on the dirt floor, hugging themselves up in their tattered apparel [sic] in an effort to keep from freezing to death. There was no fire in the little fireplace and in a box that served as a cupboard were a few but empty dishes.

Corporal Punishment in the School System

Alamo Elementary was the closest school for the Ochoas and the Carreons lying approximately four blocks northwest of the barrio sector where part of their history in the United States commenced. Barrio kids, including the Ochoas and Carreons, eagerly looked forward to the opportunity of going to school, not realizing what was in store for them once they entered the classroom environment.

Once in attendance, they were warned from the beginning that there was to be no Spanish spoken at all, and those in violation of this actual US law would face punishment. Not realizing this law was going to be enforced, I broke it many times and was paddled directly by the principal at Alamo Grammar School more than ten times each time. One of the violations was due to a need to go to the bathroom. I asked permission in Spanish to go to "el exusado" (bathroom).

Another infraction was related to recess. I took off and went home, not knowing what recess meant. A truant officer caught me sleeping inside an old abandoned car in front of the barrio apartment complex. He got me by the hair and drove me straight to the principal's office where I was paddled mercilessly.

Oscar J. Martinez in *Troublesome Border* says:

> Until the 1960s, it was common for children to be punished in schools for speaking Spanish. School officials pointed to the need to learn English as the reason for inflicting sanctions, but to Spanish speaking students the message was a devastating one: using Spanish and practicing or exhibiting Mexican cultural traits were negative forms of behavior that should be eliminated. Outside

of the schools that message was reinforced with negative characterizations of Mexicans in American popular culture.

Other punishment incidents were not always related to speaking Spanish. Maria Luisa Soltis, a retired teacher, remembers when she was a student in the 1940s at Alamo Grammar School in El Paso, "I was swatted for drinking water from the fountain that was right next to me. The teacher also scolded me for doing so without her permission."

My wife, R. Esther Valenzuela, experienced a somewhat traumatic event in first grade. Her teacher gave out crayons without any explanation to each of the students, and Esther started peeling off the labels. She remembered that she didn't think about what she was doing; perhaps she was bored and had nothing else to do. The teacher got very angry and took Esther's hands and hit her fingers with a hard wood ruler. That left Esther in shock, speechless, and motionless for what seemed to be a long time. We can only imagine what went through this six-year-old's innocent mind. From then on, Esther was scared of attending school and frightened of the teacher.

Stories are still told about a man who was the assistant principal at Alamo Grammar School and at Bowie Middle School. He carried a paddle around all the time to scare the children into obeying the rules.

One of the famous stories about punishment took place in Fabens in the early 1940s. A gas leak caused an explosion in a building next to the school during class. Most of the children left their desks and rushed to look out the windows to see what had happened. As the story goes, the commotion angered the teacher, an Anglo-American woman, and she swatted numerous children unceasingly for getting up from their seats without her permission.

It was not unusual for teachers to pull up a girl's dress for the paddling, exposing her undergarments to the rest of the class. Similarly, the boy's trousers were pulled down for his paddling. Teachers had the freedom to discipline as they thought the situation required.

A Man Named Aoy

by Conrey Bryson

ON CHRISTMAS EVE, 1890, A SIXTY-SEVEN-year-old man was on a ladder, cleaning the windows of his rented rooms, above and behind the Reckhardt Assay Office on San Francisco Street in El Paso. He slipped and fell to the icy sidewalk below, suffering a broken leg. A doctor was called, and the injured man was taken upstairs to his rooms. Dr. Baird found that the man was not only serious hurt, but was suffering badly from malnutrition. The doctor and the others soon made another discovery which was to play an important part in the educational history of El Paso.

The small quarters were equipped with seats, a blackboard, a case of books, chalk and erasers. Clearly this was a schoolroom, a fact that was soon verified by the arrival of some pupils who had learned of the incident to their beloved schoolmaster, identified as "Senior Aoy." His students were all Mexican Americans, and it was soon found that this was the only facility in boomtown El Paso for their education. City fathers and education-minded citizens were hard put to provide education for children who already spoke English. The rolls of the first public school, opened on March 5, 1883, show an enrollment of 94 pupils, and not a Spanish surname in the list.

The El Paso School Board was soon apprised of the contribution which "Professor Aoy" was making toward the education of a neglected segment of the city's population. As soon as Mr. Aoy recovered sufficiently, he was placed on the payroll; and preparations were made for establishing a school for these students. In the fall of 1892, the Mexican Preparatory School was opened, with Professor Aoy as its principal. The new school met in an old Custom House building at Third and Oregon Streets while a new building for the school was being financed and constructed. Before it could be completed, Professor Aoy passed away, in 1895. He died penniless, and the school board provided for his burial and erected a suitable headstone for his grave in Evergreen Cemetery.

It was inevitable that the new school should be called Aoy School, the name it has retained for nearly 100 years; but where did the name come from? A-O-Y is not a natural combination of Spanish letters, and it was widely speculated that this was an assumed name, possibly from the initial of his parents.

One man who tried to unravel the secrets of Aoy's background was G.W. Hare, who wrote the story of Aoy's life for *Quien Sabe*, published by El Paso High School in 1900. According to Hare's account, the subject was born in Spain of parents who belonged to nobility in Valencia. Because the young man was precocious and devoted to learning, he was assisted by Franciscan priests and studied to become a part of their order. At the age of 17 he took vows and entered a monastery; he was ordained a priest in 1854. Soon he begun to doubt some of the things he had been taught, left the order, and began a wandering career of searching for the truth. He worked for a time on the docks of Havana. There he heard favorable reports about the Mayans of Yucatan and lived among them for a time. Still not satisfied that he had found the truth, he came to United State; and in Arizona or Utah, he became acquainted with the Mormons and joined the Church of Jesus Christ of Latter-day Saints.

It is at this point that the present author's research into the Aoy story begins. In 1933, President Anthony W. Ivins, First Counselor to President Heber J. Grant of the Church of Jesus Christ of Latter-day Saints, wrote a letter to Bishop Arwell L Pierce of the El Paso Ward of his church, commonly known as Mormon Church. The pertinent part of the letter reads:

Professor A V. Joy, founder of the Joy School of El Paso was a member of the Church and died so. He was the principal translator of the Spanish edition of the *Book of Mormon*, a man of very high attainments and a splendid character so far as I have been able to determine. I was not acquainted with the man…but I knew of his work, and think that it might be…proper if we should place a marker at his grave.

Clearly the letter referred to Mr. Aoy; and Bishop Pierce, knowing of my interest in El Paso history, asked me to investigate the matter and give him my recommendations. The statement that "Professor A. V. Joy…was the principal translator of the Spanish edition of the Book of Mormon" sent me hurrying to a statement in G. W. Hare's narrative:

> He spent two years…translating the *Book of Mormon* into Spanish. He was an accomplished linguist and a born poet, and in consequence the *Book of Mormon* is a great deal better Spanish than English. Completing the work, he did not copyright it but gave it to the apostle of the Church, as he done it wholly as a labor of love, the reader may judge of the honest, confiding man's surprise, when it began to be noised about that the apostle had received a new revelation, which was nothing more than the *Book of Mormon* in classical Spanish. Once more he was disappointed in human nature. He attempted to expose a fraud, but the ignorant fanatics, the Mormons, would not listen to him. Every man who heard of it was turned against him. He could no longer live in peace among the Mormons.

This seemed entirely unreasonable. Why should a translation of the *Book of Mormon* be put forth as "a new revelation"? Did it actually happen? From William A. Lund, Assistant Church Historian, I secured a Photostat copy of the title page of the first translation of the *Book of Mormon* into Spanish. It showed the translators as Meliton G. Trejo and James Z. Stewart. No mention of Aoy.

I located Meliton G. Trejo's son, who was then Bishop of the St. David Ward, St. David, Arizona. Bishop Trejo described his father as a well-educated Spaniard who had served as a missionary in Mexico with his companion translator, James Z. Stewart. But the Bishop knew nothing of Aoy?

Then the question arose: If Aoy was an assumed name, as many supposed, what name was the man using in Utah? Trenial Pauly, First Counselor to Bishop Pierce, found a new clue. He located an elderly Mexican woman who told him that Aoy's real name was Jaime Vila. At that point, Archibald F. Bennett, Secretary of the Genealogical Society of Utah, was not most helpful. In the records of the Mormon temple in Logan, Utah, he found the following record of sacred ordinances performed on November 3, 1884:

> Name: Jaime Aoy Olives Vila
> Born: 24 Mar, 1823, Mahon, Menorca, Spain
> Father: Jaime Vila (born Villa Carlos, Menorca)
> Mother: Margarete Olivares

One thing seemed certain—if Aoy was an assumed name, it was assumed at the time of his birth.

Still unanswered was the question of Aoy's connection, if any, with the Spanish translation of the Book of Mormon. Then, in 1980, the Church News section of the Salt Lake City Desert news published an article about the translation, stating that Trejo and Stewart had received valuable assistance from a "Brother Aoy." I rushed a letter to Gordon Irving, Research Historian of the Church Historical Department. He responded, enclosing copies of two letters which answered the question.

The first was a letter dated July 15, 1884, from Moses Thatcher, member of the Council of Twelve Apostles of the Church, to John Taylor, President of the Church. After reporting that the Spanish translation of the *Book of Mormon* was ready for the press, the letter read:

> Brother Aoy…has assisted in the final revision of the translation and…besides being thoroughly educated in his own language (the Spanish) is an editor of considerable experience and a practicable printer. He is now out of employment so that we can secure his services both as proof reader and tipho [sic], should you decide to go on with the publication at once…I hardly know how we can get along with the printing without the assistance of Brother Aoy…

Aoy's name spelled correctly in the letter of January 19, 1885, from George Q. Cannon, First Counselor to President Taylor, to James Z. Stewart, one of the translators of the Spanish edition.

The first pages of the *Book of Mormon* in Spanish are in the hands of the printers, and Brother Aoy has read the proofs and has suggested several changes. He suggests the use of placas, all through the book for the word used by us in English-plates instead of placas, which is sometimes used in the translation…and which, he says, means "medals." He also says that the word anales is used for "record" a large number of times, which he says is the correct word, but the word recuerdos is used twice, and, as he says, incorrectly. In the last sentence of the testimony of the three witnesses, where the words La Gloria are used, he would substitute el honor…

There are several other corrections…which I do not think necessary to enumerate here, there being two or three instances where he suggests the use of the singular instead of the plural, it being singular in English. There are also, he says, several changes in the termination of words, by which the tense is changed.

Apparently all the suggested changes were acceptable to translator Stewart, for the present edition of the *Libro de Mormon* contains all of them. Clearly Aoy was of major assistance in translating the book into Spanish. Equally clearly, he was not the sole nor chief translator. There is no evidence in the Church archives of any quarrel between Aoy and others involved in the translation. There is no record that Aoy ever left the Church, and it may well be as stated in the letter from Anthony W. Ivins quoted earlier, that he was "a member of the Church and died so."

There yet remained the request from President Ivins that the local Church place a memorial marker at Aoy's grave. I had stood at his grave one April 27, the anniversary of his death, and watched a group of girls and boys from Aoy School place flowers at his grave and hear the words of tribute from their teacher. Reporting to Bishop Pierce, I stated my opinion that no better tribute could be devised than the one already carved on his tombstone:

O. V. Aoy
EL MAESTRO DE LA ESCUELA
NACIO EN LA ESPAÑA, A.D. 1822
Y MURIO EN EL PASO, TEXAS APRIL 27,
1895
"y respondiendo el Rey, los dira:
De cierto os digo que en cuanto los
hiciesteis a uno de estos, mis hermanos
pequenistos, a mi lo hecisteis."

San Mateo, Chapter 40

In English, the familiar words from St. Matthew are: "and the King shall answer and say unto them: insomuch as ye have done it unto one of the least of these, My brethren, ye have done unto me."

1. G.W. Hare, "The Life and Character of Olivas Villanueva Aoy," *Quien Sabe,* Vol. I, No. 8, May, 1900. Monthly publication of El Paso High School. Hare was evidently the editor, since his initials, "G.W.H.," appear after the editorial. Copy in the Southwest Reference Department, El Paso Public Library.
2. Elaine Lewis Morrel, *The Rise and Growth of Education in El Paso, Texas*, Masters Thesis, University of Texas, 1936, 40–50.
3. Bertha Archer Schaer, *Historical Sketch of Aoy School*, El Paso Public Schools, April 27, 1951, 3–7.
4. Hare.
5. Ivins to Pierce, May 11, 1933. In possession of author.
6. Lund to Bryson. August, 1937.
7. Trejo to Bryson, August 1937.
8. Bennett to Bryson, July 19, 1943.
9. Irving to Bryson, December 17, 1980.
10. Thatcher to Taylor, July 15, 1884. Archives, Church of Jesus Christ of Latter-day Saints, Salt Lake City, Utah.

11. Cannon to Stewart, January 19, 1885. Archives, Church of Jesus Christ of Latter-day Saints, Salt Lake City, Utah.
12. Lds.org "Pioneers in every Land . . . Unto these the least" recommended video to "The story of OLIVAS AOY."

Alamo Elementary School (South El Paso).

Academic Discriminatory Measures against Immigrants (1920–1926)

Mario García in *Desert Immigrants* explains that although Mexican children attended American schools and, in many cases, were encouraged to do so, that it "did not alter in general the educational discrimination and racial segregation that was aimed at Mexican children in El Paso and that reinforced a lower rate of economic advancement for the Mexican working class." Clearly, Mexicans have not had a history of educational neglect but a history of limited schooling, which has, in turn, supported the desire of southwestern employers for menial, cheap, and manageable labor.

A teacher at Beall Elementary School in El Paso with 100 percent Mexican students gave this advice to a group of students who were finishing sixth grade in 1920: "(Do not) plan on going to high school because Mexicans only work as laborers. You people are here to dig ditches and use a pick and shovel." (Note: One of the six graders who heard this advice but did not heed it was Guillermo Balderas. Guillermo grew up to be a religious leader and the first Mexican bishop for the Church of Jesus Christ of Latter-day Saints in South El Paso.)

The foundation for this discrimination began many years earlier when the first schools opened in El Paso during the 1880s and only a few Mexican students attended. Their failure to attend was attributed to several situations: they couldn't speak English, their poverty, and the fact that their labor was needed at home. In the late 1880s, Olivas V. Aoy began teaching English to these children so they would be able to enter school. His efforts, as we know, made him famous and eventually brought about the famous Aoy Elementary School.

Even by the 1950s, discriminatory practices were still prevalent when I was in school. An eighth-grade diploma was considered the end of school for many students of Mexican origin. The basic reason for that was because they had to earn a living and help the family. That limited education, however, created the belief that their capacity to learn was limited, and that, in turn, created more discrimination. In my case, I was placed in vocational training to learn wood working, but for me, that did not affect my ambition to graduate from high school at all costs. Also, my wife's parents, Guadalupe and Elena Piñón, were fervent believers in education despite their minimal education at the elementary level in Mexico. They instilled their values in their children, who all achieved significant success.

Elizabeth obtained her Masters and became a high school Counselor, Esther graduated with a degree in Bilingual Educationj, Arturo also obtained his Masters and became an assistant school Principal, Gloria received her degree in Mathematics and taught high school for decades, Helen came out Salutatorian in her high school, Guadalupe "Wally" became a diplomat with the State Department in Washington D.C.

My parents had always hoped that someday, at least, one of their children would graduate from high school. As it turned out, I was the only one who graduated, and I was the youngest. All of my brothers and sisters dropped out of school between the seventh and eleventh grade.

Most parents thought that continuing education beyond high school was a ridiculous idea. It probably never crossed their minds that their own children could possibly achieve a higher level of education. Perhaps due to poor educational circumstances in Mexico, immigrant parents in the barrio found it ludicrous for their kids to spend time and energy on that matter. They encouraged their kids to concentrate, for the most part, on the reality of working to help support and contribute to the family's economic condition. It was generally believed that educational aspirations beyond the seventh grade were reserved for those with economic advantage and the intellectual English-speaking sectors elsewhere in society. At the seventh grade level, many students from the barrio went to work at any menial jobs they could find or joined the military.

Bowie High School.

Guadalupe Valdéz, in her book *Con Respecto*, gives insight into the misunderstandings, assumptions, miscommunication, and expectations of those times:

> For the children, the teachers, and the parents, the school context presented many challenges. Teachers tried their best and appeared to fail. Children brought with them skills they had learned at home and found them inappropriate. Parents felt helpless, confused, and angry.
>
> Both the schools and the families made assumptions about each other. Schools expected a "standard" family, a family whose members were educated, who were familiar with how schools worked, and who saw their role as complementing the teacher's in developing children's academic abilities. It did not occur to school personnel that parents might not know the appropriate ways to communicate with the teachers, that they might feel embarrassed about writing notes filled with errors, and that they might not even understand how to interpret their children's report cards.

> When children came to school without certain skills that their families, in good faith, believed the teachers should teach (e.g., the alphabet, the colors, the numbers), school personnel assumed parental indifference, troubled homes, and little interest in education.
>
> The parents, on the other hand, were living lives that required large amounts of energy just to survive. They had little formal schooling and few notions about what schools expected of them and their children. (p. 167)

Despite the unfortunately high school dropout rates in the 1940s—1960s, some students did pursue academic routes. My cousin, Samuel "Sammy" Carreon, was the model student in the barrio. Sammy graduated salutatorian in his high school class and thereafter received a degree in engineering. During one part of his career, he was the chief engineer for the State of Alaska. Similarly, I chose to continue my educational aspirations and graduated from high school and eventually completed studies at the University of Texas at El Paso, and participated in continuing employment, training, and management development at Memphis State University, University of Northern Colorado, University of Utah, Pan American University, Wabash and Salt Lake Community Colleges, etc.

The Arrival of Television and its Impact on Entertainment in El Paso

The arrival of television in the 1950s was a most eventful period of time for people in the barrio. Television had a powerful effect and opened up a new world within the barrio. It was magical. Even though the picture quality was primitive and lacked sound, it was given a tremendous welcome by the people in South El Paso. It was an exhilarating experience. The effects were great and changed the scenario in the barrio tremendously. The implication was that people no longer had to wait until Saturdays to go downtown to see movies.

Television brought weekly entertainment into the homes of those who could afford it. The Ochoas and the Carreones struggled for some time until each family had their own black-and-white programmed unit. The Bellah family was the first to purchase a television. They prided themselves on inviting some of the kids to watch the small amount of shows available back then. Mainly wrestling, Western movies, and some cartoons.

Prior to television, people spent twenty cents to go inside movie theaters, which also entitled them to a bag of popcorn and a soda pop or candy, all for the amazing cost of only twenty cents! After the movies, people flocked to view Los Lagartos or Cocodrilos (alligators) at La Plaza de los Lagartos or San Jacinto Plaza located in downtown El Paso. (City officials cracked down on people who abused the crocodiles by throwing stones and other objects at them. The crocodiles were doomed to be removed and placed in the Zoo at Washington Park.)

THE SALSA CULTURE INVADES AMERICA

Plaza de Los Lagarto. Alligator Plaza in downtown El Paso.

Apart from the attraction of the alligators, the lighting of the Christmas tree in San Jacinto Plaza was the only other exciting event worth watching, especially during the holidays.

There were many movie houses in downtown El Paso in those days. They included the Plaza, the Crawford, the Allanay, the State Theatre, the Palace, and El Calzetin (the sock) and the Colon for Spanish speakers. The cost per movie was ten cents, the popcorn was five cents, and soda drinks were five cents. The movies and the alligators in San Jacinto Plaza occupied us kids practically all day Saturday from morning to evening. We watched the same movies over and over until it was time to go home at night.

The Plaza Theatre was by far the most popular and most enjoyable place to enter. The interior had a beautiful ornateness. The majestically constructed ceiling was the most talked about aspect of the theatre. Attendees were treated to an imaginary adventure. When they were sitting in their seats, they could look up and see what appeared to be stars in the middle of the dark ceiling! That and the addition of music from the organ created a thrilling and wondrous experience for the audience in the Plaza theatre. The first movie ever presented in Cinemascope color inside the Plaza Theatre was *The House of Wax* with Vincent Price.

The Calzetin and the Colon theaters presented movies in Spanish only. The Calzetin Theater was mostly geared for the benefit of the poor who could not afford entry into other theatres. Foul smell was the immediate and most distinguishing feature of the Calzetin, but we kids never complained.

During the week after school, lots of kids went to the Bellahs to watch the only television in the barrio. The Bellahs soon got tired of having all the neighborhood kids in their apartment, and decided not to let them come and watch any more. Later on, another family bought a television and after school, all the kids would run as fast as possible to be first in line outside the screen door to try and get a glimpse of the television inside. However, the family was rude and did not welcome kids at all, and they kept kids from forming lines outside their apartment by throwing water through the door's screen.

Television improved and programs were telecast in almost perfect black and white with good sound. Popular programs bombarded South El Paso: the *Hit Parade*, the *Mickey Mouse Club*, *Lassie*, *Live Wrestling*, *Science Fiction Theater*, *The Millionaire*, and the daily news on KROD Channel 4, PBS Channel 13, and KTSM Channel 9, Steve Crosno's *Sock Hop*, *Uncle Roy Show*, the *Ed Sullivan Show*, *The Honeymooners*, *I Love Lucy*, *Mission Impossible*, the *Twilight Zone*, and *Bonanaza* along with all kinds of soap operas. Radio became a thing of the past replaced forever by television. From then on, television viewing kept kids up late into the night and interfered with their homework and other responsibilities at home.

The Gangs of South El Paso and the Pachuco

Fred Morales in his book *El Segundo Barrio* says that the gangs of South El Paso were…named mostly after the streets on which they lived or hung around. (For example) The 4Fs were on Mesa Street, the Little 9ers and the Lucky 13s were at Fifth and Oregon Streets, the 14s were at Fourth and St. Vrain Streets, the Parkers were on Park Street, the 13-9s were at Kansas and Fourth Streets, the 7-Xs were on Seventh Street and the 10s were at Park and Tenth Streets.

Other gangs were the King Gamblers, Golden Jewels, Fatimas, Lads and Mads, Rhythm Devils, Little 10s, Rebels, T.P.M.., KKs, (King) Cobras, and the Happy Wanderers. The 14s and the 7-Xs were allied, and (they) controlled a good part of South El Paso and the other side was controlled by the Lucky 13s and the 13-9s.

Most gang members now began to wear baggy pants with pegged ankles to roam the streets with chains hung from the belt of the pocket in a long loop. They are now called also boogies, zoot suiters or pachucos. The term "pachuco" originated in the South El Paso barrios of Chihuahuita and the Segundo Barrio.

Rafael Jesus González, author of *Pachuco: The Birth of a Creole Language*, says that the pachucos came into existence as a subculture group. "The evolution of its language is an area of study that has hardly been tapped, yet which, I believe, can throw much light on our culture and the evolution and uses of language.

The name pachuco has been the source of much discussion for the investigators of this group because of the difficulty in tracing the word to its source and origin. Presbítero Canuto E. Anaya makes mention of the word "pachoa-can" (also "pachu-can") of Náhuatl origin roughly translated as "residence of the chief." Other Mexican linguists, Cecilio A. Robelo and Dávila Garabí, on the other hand, maintain that the word means "grassy place" from the Náhuatl words *pachtli* (grass or hay) and *ca* (place of). Haldeen Braddy suggests that the word may come from a corruption of the Spanish "pachucho," adjective meaning overripe, almost spoiled. I myself tend to agree with Mr. George C. Barker that it simply comes from the colloquial way of saying El Paso, the city in which the pachucos originated as a subculture in its own right.

Tin Tan, Mexican comedian,
the original pachuco.

Beatrice Griffith, in her book *American Me*, however, finds that "the term [pachuco] seems to have been applied colloquially to Mexican-American youths and their families coming from El Paso on the crest of one of the great migratory waves to California in the early twenties."

Gabriel Córdova, several years court interpreter for the El Paso police court, in a letter to Dr. Barker says that the jargon originated with a group of marijuana smokers and peddlers.

Mr. Ramón Villalobos, police reporter for the *El Paso Times*, maintains that in the 1940s, the pachucos settling in Los Angeles formed their gangs and warfare broke between the native gangs of the Califas and the newly arrived pachucos. The Califas, upon suffering defeat, adopted the name pachuco for their own designation. In any event, the pachucos were a force that moved rapidly from El Paso's west and quickly spread its jargon throughout that part of the United States.

In June 1943, the word "pachuco" became nationally known because of the riots that took place in the Los Angeles County. These riots involved several Pachuco gangs and members of the US armed forces stationed in the Los Angeles area. The notoriety of those riots was all too well spread, but the reasons given for them too simple and varied to tell us much. The best study of the riots is the penetrating chapter "The Zootsuit Riots" in Ms. Griffith's book. Ms. Griffith puts them in their context of war hysteria, fear, and tension. But those along with the pachuco habits of dress (the zoot suit); tattooing on the hands, arms, and face; incidence of delinquency; and peculiar argot gave rise to the Pachuco legend exaggerating the group's harmfulness and culpability.

The pachuco impacted El Paso in the 1930s and 1940s and gave meaning to its subculture in the introduction of a new dictionary of language influenced to a significant degree by "el caló" (the jargon of the Spanish gypsy much used by the bullfighters), Hispanicized English, Anglicized Spanish, and words of pure invention interspersed with words from the Náhuatl and held together by faulty Spanish sentence construction and grammar.

Pachuco Slang from the Barrio

chante – home (from Náhuatl home)
cantón – chante, home
garras – clothes (rags)
el mono – movies (monkey; in New Mexico it means cartoon)
rolar – to sleep (to roll in circular motion; in New Mexico: to lie down)
una rola – a song
tacuche – suit or dress (from Náhuatl: to bind with cloth)
cahuquear – to double cross (from "cahuco," in Mexico: a counterfeit coin, probably origination from Náhuatl)
birria – double meaning: a meat dish or barbecue meat, beer
vatobato – boy, man
chavala (muchacha) – girl
tando (sombrero) – hat
calcos (zapatos) – shoes
lima (camisa) – shirt
vato/bato, vata/bata – dude, guy, girl (originally an old, "bata" in New Mexico meant clownish, also means sweetheart)
jefe/jefa – father, mother (originally a chief), boss
chuchuluco – candy (from Náhuatl; means a gross, disagreeable person in New Mexico)
caméo – work
trucha – watch out, lookout
biroles – beans, frijóles
anda en pelota – he (she) is walking around naked
bofo – idiotic, stupid
un pisto – a drink
dátil – fruit of the date palm "date"
ganga – a bargain or deal, mostly associated with a gang
mecha – a wick, match

chanza – an amusing saying or act, chance
carro – a cart, car
bote – "can", mostly associated with jail
chueco – crooked, illegal
quebrada – to give one a break, flexible, opportunity; ("dar quebrada": to give a break)
huesos – bones or dice
lechuga – "lettuce" dollars
patada – a kick, thrill; e.g., agarrar patada – to get a kick at something
papel – paper, newspaper
monquiar – to monkey around
bonque – bunk
daime – dime
un bola – a dollar bill
un toleco – fifty-cent piece
la perinola, la chora, la chirula – the penis/dick or testicle area
un nicle – a nicle
waino – "wino"
deaquea – okay
chequiar – to check
chitiar – to cheat
guachar – to look at or watch
flonquear – to flunk
mistiar – to miss
parquiar – to park
pápiro – paper
chutiar – to shoot
ponchar – to punch
brecas – breaks
espiche – speech
chainar – to shine
bonchi(e) – bunch
yarda – yard, as in back yard
dichar – to ditch
chain – shine

tíquete – ticket
tichár – to teach
fonis – newspaper funnies or cartoons
suera – sweater
las jainas – the girls, girlfriends or sweethearts
el jaino – the guy, boyfriend
la lira – guitar
puto cabrón – damn stupid male gay, girlish, lost cause
joto – male attracted to men or the lack of masculinity
puta – lesbian (female), to some extent heterosexual
mamflor – male gay, attracted to men
mariposa – lack of masculinity, gay, girlish
el filero – a knife
la chompa – the head
la ruca – old lady, live-in girlfriend
mi ruca – my old lady, wife
las washas – rings, washers
carnál – brother or close friend, associate
la ficha – money
la lana – money
la roña – cracked dry hands, dirty beyond help
el carpo – carpenter
la carrucha, la ramfla – car (from wheelbarrow)
refinar – eat food
un alambrazo – telephone or a wired message
zorreando or huachando – watching, looking up, "I'm keeping you under a watchful eye"
la ramfla – the car
Esta ramfla es una tartana – This car is old (infers the first Ford car built in the 1900s)

The development of the pachuco's el caló revolutionized the barrio Spanish. It was incorporated into the daily life of the Mexican immigrant and contained a more colorful and expressive language considered by many people then, and even now, as low class. Despite its powerful entry into the barrio, it has never become entirely acceptable by the more cultured and educated people as tools to good communication. The effect of pachuco's language in Mexico was negative. It was viewed as a threat to society just like the black jive or the cholo culture today. Nevertheless, it has survived the onslaught of the ages. It is not unusual to hear the pachuco jargon automatically employed in conversations by the descendants of those who experienced living in the barrio during the 1940s–1960s. It is still used in bilingual as well as monolingual homes of today by los batos (dudes) or homeboys who are survivors of the pachuco era. In continuation, consider the Pachuco language contractions:

"Vamos a echarnos un taco" – Let's go eat a bite
"Se me fue la onda" – I forgot
"No seas hocicón" – Don't be a bad mouth
"Vamos a camellar" – Let's go to work
"Ay te huacho" – See you later
"Pórtate bien sino te va agarrar el chamuco" – Behave or the devil is going to get you
"No te hagas él maje" – Don't act dumb or don't lie to me
"ojo de acha" – keep an eye
"Simon que sí" – Yes, you bet
"Lo hice pendejo" – I tricked the dummy, I fooled him
"Vamos al Chuco" – let's go to El Paso; "Voy pa' el Chuco (Pachuco?)"
"Me siento deaquea" – I feel great
"Llevatela suave o deaquea" – Take it easy
"Como fregas el alma" – You are bothersome, Don't bother me
"No te hagas el sonso o el maje" – Don't play dumb with me
"Están suave las tablitas ese" – Your shoes (pointed at the front) are nice looking, dude
"tanto pedo para cagar aguado – waste of time, lots of bull, or work for nothing
"Me escamó" – He scared me
"No vayas a chismear" – Don't squeal
"No la levantas" – You're not good enough
"Se lo llevaron a la pinta" – They took him to prison

"Mira ese tirili" – Look at that hoodlum
"Me meti en una bronca" – I got into trouble
"Le echaron la tierra encima" – They destroyed him, He lost, They got rid of him
"No seas gacho" – Don't be stupid/mean/insensitive
"Usa la chompa menso" – Use your head, dummy; Think straight, stupid
"No seas marrano" – Don't try to trick me, Don't be crooked, Deal with me straight (marrano is associated with dirty pig)
"Ya se ranó el güey" – The dummy got married
"Chinga tu madre cabrón" – Damn your mother, stupid lowlifer
"Tiendete, ay, vienen los juras" – take off quick, here comes the police
"Me arranqué" – I took off quick
"Se me fue la onda" – I literally forgot
"Ojo, ese bato es pirujo" – Watch out! That dude is gay
"Callate el hocico" – Shut your mouth
"Me la rayó" – He (she) said bad words about me
"Me rayó la madre" – He damn me using my mother (madre is mother)
"Es pinacate" – He's black
"Es una víbora" – He (she) is treacherous
"Alguien me echó la sal" – Somebody condemned me or cast an evil action against me
"Se fue a pistear" – He (She) went drinking or went to get drunk
"Echame una mano" – Give me a hand, Help me
"Que agüite" – Doggone it
"Cortate tus pedos" – Cut the bull, Talk to me straight, Stop, Quit it
"son un chirinoleo" – bunch of liars, untruthful talker
"Esta chispeando" – It's starting to rain
"No la muelas" – Don't mess things up
"Me pescó la Migra" – The border patrol caught me
"Es de los otros" – He (She) is a gay person
"Me quité los pantas" – I took off my pants
"Estás malo de la cola" – You're wrong or sick in the behind

"Préstame una lana" – Lend me some money

"Le dieron aire" – They fired him (her)

chaqueteando – turncoat, traitor or turn against

"El que lo huele, debajo lo trae" – If he (she) smells it, he's (she) got it behind him (her)

"No me metas en tus pedos" – Don't get me involved in your problems

"Ay vienen los cachuchones" – Here comes the police/border patrol

"Alivianame" – Give me a hand/help me with some money

"Voy a volar a califa" – I am going to fly to California

"Dame esa chiva" – Give me that thing or hand me that item (chiva associated with goat)

"este atascado" – dirty, filthy, or dummy, stupid

"Estás malo de la cola" – You're stupid/You're ignorant as hell

"Que te pica" – What is bothering you/What's your problem

"Te estoy tanteando" – I am watching you very carefully/I am keeping a close eye on you

"¿Porqué te estás curando de mi? – Why are you laughing at me/insulting me/mocking me

"Están tocando mi rola favorita" – They are playing my favorite song

"No seas huevón" – Don't be lazy ("huevón" refers to eggs or a man's testicles)

"Chingadera" – Damn thing

"una changada" – group of monkeys

"Esa huisa tiene buen mofle" – That girl has a good gluteus maximus.

"Estuve con las huisas" – I was with the girls (associated with girls of the night/prostitutes)

"Nos dimos una chinga" – We worked very hard

"Ya se ranó" – He (she) got married

"¿Vas a arrear tu?" – Are you going to drive?

"¡Que carta!" – You look nice!

"Es mayate/pinacate" – He is black

"El güey se la mascó" – He found out the stupid way

"No seas güey – Don't be stupid

"Largate o te doy un patadón" – get out of here or I'll kick you

"Te voy a patear sino te la cortas" – I'm going to kick if you don't stop

"Callate o te sueno" – Shut up or I'll hit you/I'll spank you

"¡A toda madre!" – That's great!

"Me estás toriqueando" – You're putting me on, Bull, You're hiding something from me

la vaisa – the hand

"Me tiró un dedo" – He threw a finger at me

"Echár un bolado" – Flip a coin

chillón – crybaby

chiple – spoiled

la huacha – clock or wristwatch

las huachas – a horseshoe-like throwing game using washers

"Trais un frájo?" – Got a cigarette?

"Tira esa vacha" – Throw that cigarette butt away

"Trucha" – Be on the lookout

"Es muy trucha, cuidado" – He is cunning, watch out, avoid him

A huevo – Of course or else, derived from "stubbornness"

el chusco – movie (from Tin Tan the comedian)

"Trais una quira? – Can you spare a quarter?

nicle – nickle

la chora – the penis

"Ese cuate es muy mamon y lambion" – That dude likes to score brownie points, hiding behind somebody's laurels for protection and security, maybe trying to gain an advantage over someone else by using his (hers) prestigious standing in the barrio

"Se te ven las lonjas de tu panza" – Your fat belly is showing

"Te sales vato/bato" – You're way off base, dude; Your thinking is out of touch

Totacho – English

tarugo – dummy, ignorant

guaje – stupid

la pipiluya – tip money, free for all, gratuity, money thrown at an audience of kids

"Pasame un aventón" – Give me a ride

"No la rieges" – Don't screw things, don't mess up, do it right

"Vive chole" – Be quiet

la lisa – the shirt

butí loco – Very crazy, absurd, or out of his mind

"Le suena el coco" – He's crazy/dumb/out of his mind

"Le suena la chompa" – He's crazy in the head

"Es Mojado Juareño" – He's a wetback from Juarez, Mexico

"Está malo del culo ese güey" – That stupid guy is lying/acting dumb

"No te hagas el maje" – Don't act dumb

"Es una rata/ratero" – He's a crook/thief

"Está Chingao (do)" – He's beyond hope and help; contraction intended to hurt the destitute, poor, and hopeless—a common and demeaning bad expression

el toilido – the john, toilet

chichón – swollen bump resulting from injury to the head

"No seas gacho" – Don't be mean, Be cool

"Mochate" – Give me half, Hand it over

"Chispas" – Dang, I goofed

"No la muelas" – Don't screw it up, Don't mess things up

"En la torre!" – oh, oh, I (we) had it coming

"Se me Arrancó" – It was more than I expected, I got into trouble

"Se Arrancó" – He took off

"Trae la chora parada" – His penis is erect

"¡Te voy a poner la Pompa andar!" – I'm going to beat you up!

"No hagas pedo" – Be quiet, Don't say anything, Keep your mouth shut or else

"Se méo los pantalones" – He wet his pants

ñeango – useless, slow, hopeless

"No te apures, la riega todo el tiempo" – Don't worry, He (she) messes things up all the time

"Ay vine la llorona por ti" – Here comes the ghost of the weeping lady after you

"A huevo quiere ir" – He insists on going no matter what!

"Me cais gordo" – You turn me off, I can't stand you ("gordo" is equivalent to fat)

"Me agarraron en las moras" – I was caught red handed, they caught me on the act

"No vayas a chisquearla" – Don't mess things up

"Voy echarme una playa" – I'm taking a shower

"Tanto pedo para cagar aguado!" – All this worrying or commotion for nothing!

"Se viste como un tirili" – He dresses like a pachuco

"No seas resongón" – Don't back talk to me

flaco talaco – skinny

"Está pelón esto" – This is difficult/impossible

"Voy a tirar el agua" – I'm going to take a leak

"Te van a robar la cantina" – They're going to steal from your bar/your zipper is open

"Se Ranó"– He (She) got married

"Voy a arrear" – I'm going to drive

"¡Que carta!" – You look darn nice!

"Anda en muy malas ondas" – He's in real serious trouble, He's on the pathway to problems

"Pasame los calcos" – Give me the shoes

"Me voy a patín" – I'm walking, I have no ride

"Echate un trago" – Have a drink

"Ya me voy al chante" – I'm going home now

"Donde están los calzas? – Where's the socks?

"Se surró en los calzones" – He (She) did poopoo/number two in his panties/underwear

"Me torcieron" – The cops got me, I'm in trouble with the law

los juras – the policemen or cops

"Me metieron en la pinta" – I was incarcerated or I ended up in prison

"No seas guey" – Don't be stupid

"ese vato/bato bofo no la levanta porque es un pendejo"– that stupid dude/guy is stupid/ worthless and dumb

"No te hagas pendejo" – Don't act dumb/act innocent, You stupid fool

"Chinga tu madre cabrón" – Damn your mom, you idiot

"Lo mareriaron al pinchi guey" – They fooled that stupid idiot

chingao – damn thing

"No seas culero" – Don't be a stupid asshole

güey – dummy, ignorant, stupid

biroles – beans

"Me agarraron en las moras - Caught me red-handed doing what I was doing wrong

"Andan Moros en la costa" - Watch out! Someone is watching or spying on us

"No sabe como chiflar el pendejo" – The dummy doesn't know how to whistle

"Andale nalga huanga" - Come on, you slowpoke flappy ass

"Mi ruca me dejo" - My old woman (wife) left me

Other Pachuco Slang Words

"Se peló" – He (She) left abruptly

"Me hizo una bola de preguntas" – He asked me a lot of questions

"No la hagas llorona" – Don't make a big fuss over it, Get over it, Don't overdo it

puchale –push it

"Este cuate le macanea y se avienta" – This guy works hard and is good at what he does

"El patrón me da mucha carrilla" – The boss makes me work a lot, He's a slave driver

"Es carrillero" – He's a slave driver, He works you to death, a workaholic boss

"Anda este bato todo trolis" – This dude is not in his good mind, He's drunk/disoriented

"Le dieron aire" – He got fired

"Lo tronaron a balazos" – They killed him with lots of bullets

"Garrotearon al picher" – They bombarded the pitcher with lots of hits

"Préstame una quira" – Lend me a quarter

"Se volo la barda" – He hit a homerun

esponje - angry, mad, upset

"Se lo estraiquearon" – They struck him out

"Ando crudo" – I have a hangover

"Pura tórica" – Lots of untruthful talk

"Es conchudo" – He is deceptive/not trustworthy

"Hay viene la birula" – Here comes the crossed-eyed girl

"Es una tartan" – It's an old beat-up vehicle

"Plánchame los pantas" – Iron my pants

"Tiene una lisa a todo dar" - He (She) has a good-looking shirt

"Me escamó" – He (She) scared me

"Se me fue la onda" – I forgot

"Que aguite" – darn

"Está fregado" – He (She) is disabled/unable to perform, Down on his luck, He (She) has a bleak future, financially or economically weak

"Préstame tu ramfla" – let me borrow your car

"Está malo de la cola" – He's lying up to his butt/untruthful

"La jaina está guenota" – the girl is very sexy, sexually attractive

"Dame esa chiva" – Give me that thing (chiva derived from the name goat)

"Te van a robar la cantina" – Your zipper is open, They're going to steal your goods

Es muy chismoso - He's a pathological liar, He lies a lot

Es muy chismosa - She's a liar, She lies a lot

"Cuidado! Es muy chueco" – Beware/Be careful. He's not truthful in his dealings, untrustworthy

"Hay vienen los juras" – Here comes the police

"Hay vienen los chotas" – Here comes the police

"Este es mi chante" – This is my house

"Ya estiró las patas" - He died, His legs are stiff

"Chanza que si" – Maybe so, Perhaps yes

"No seas bruto" – Don't be a dummy, Don't be stupid

"Cuidado con él, trai el chumuco – Watch it! He's possessed of the devil, he's evil and is extremely upset

"Puro chirinol aquí" - Too much talk here based on rumors

puto – homosexual, gay

"Es de los otros" – He's from the other ones (a gay person)

pendejo cabron – stupid idiot

"La rege" – I goofed, I committed something wrong

"Me la rayó" – He said a very bad word against me, He cursed me

"Le apañas?" – You understand? You get it?

"Es muy agarrado" – He is very stingy, selfish

"Es muy agarrada" – She is very stingy, selfish

tacañio – stingy, selfish

"Le apañias?" – You get it? Do you understand?

la mordida – under-the-table handling of money, a piece of the action financially (in Mexico, it

was customary for policemen to seek a mordida in order for traffic violators to avoid fines by paying the mordida)

"Has me la parada" – tell a little white lie for me, make an exception for my sake

"Estoy canica de esa bata" – I'm infatuated and in love with that girl

"Ya se ranó" – He (She) got hitch (married)

"La chisqeo" – He (She) it screwed up, He (She) messed it up

chingao! – damn!

"Me doy" – I give up

"Metí la pata" – I screwed up, I got involved in something not pertaining to me, It was none of

my business

"Le madrugé" – I was there earlier than expected in the morning

"Anda despertando gallos" – He (She) is an early bird, He (She) woke up the roosters/woke

people earlier than expected

"Un buen gallo canta en cualquier gallinero" – If you're good at anything, you'll do good anywhere

"Es mariguano" – He's a marijuana user, an undesirable individual, We distrust him, Beware of him

"No hay pedo" – no problem! (pedo means fart)

"No hagas pedo" – Don't get over excited, Calm down, Shut up, Stop it now, no cause for rumors

"Se lo llevaron a la pinta" – They took him to jail or prison

"Es puro borlote" – It's a bunch of bull/not true, It's a lie or complete nonsense

"Estoy amolado" – I'm in a jam/a tough spot, I'm in an economical or financial circumstance, I'm ruined, I have no way out

"Es una vibora" – an astute cunning female (a snake), untrustworthy, out to do no good, adversely manipulative

"Me voy a parquear" – I'm going to park my vehicle

"Es un joto" – He's gay

jotingo – gay, homosexual

"Te doy dos llantas nuevas por una vieja" – I'll give two new tires for an old one (girl or woman)

"Te voy a dar por toda la madre" – I'm gonna whip your ass/ beat you up

ATM (a toda madre) – Great news! I like it! Exciting!

"Todavía tienes pege" – You still attract the opposite sex, charming, appealing

"Ya no la soplas" – There's no life in you, You no longer attract the opposite sex!

"Ese bato es muy huevon" – That dude is very lazy

"No tiene huevos ese bato" – That dude has no balls/no courage, He's afraid/insecure

"Llevatela suave" – Take it easy

"Se la lambio" – He (she) got what he (she) deserved.

"Me cais gordo (gorda)." – (gordo or gorda are obsessed people) I can't stand you! I dislike you, I will have no part with you, you overdo it, end of conversation.

"Vamos al Chuco"—Let's Go to El Paso

I am from El Chuco, and this is the way it was in the 1950s and 1960s!

You knew Coach Nemo Herrera (Bowie High School Hall of Fame baseball coach); Coach Kayo; Coach Rosas (who always carried a paddle to intimidate students); El Nolan (Richardson, the only coach to win three national titles: Jr. College, NIT, NCAA); el Coach Baty (Football Coach who died in an accident en el Paisano Street); la Peyton Packing Company; el Duchene (track and football star); el Hector Porras (Bowie football quarterback); el Memo Olivas, el Changoli, el Bobby y Lefty Rodriguez (legendary baseball players), el Angel Valero (valedictorian of his Bowie High class); el Sammy Carreon (salutatorian next to Angel Valero); el Paco; (Carrasco, All-State Basketball Player); Skidmore field; la Bowie Bakery; el Boy's Club; la Frontera swimming pool; la Aoy school, y la San Jacinto (elementary schools); Ben's Tacos; la Paloma Restaurant; las quermeces de St. Ignatius Church; Deras Cleaners; la ticher (teacher) Willis (Bowie), el Mr. Frank Pollitt (principal at Bowie High School, and Mr. Patton (assistant principal at Alamo and Bowie), the three swatted more kids than anyone else in barrio history); el Hortex y el Billy the Kid (manufacturers of jeans), la Farah; la Tornillo (Street); el T&P (railroad); el Rio Bravo (Rio Grande); el Alamito Center; Don Tomas Grocery; la Houchen (clinic); el Mackey del 7X (barrio gangster); el Tula (inspirational barrio coach/activist); el Mario Montes (Olympic star); el Isaac Camacho (first US soldier to escape from a North Vietnam prisoner of war camp); los Mineros campeones de Texas Western College (the Miners, 1966 NCAA First All-Black Basketball Team Champions); tacos de Salamayuca (sold in downtown El Paso on Saturdays).

Let's go to the hop del DJ Steve Crosno, "Battle of the Bands," el Jalisco Restaurant, la Frontera supermarket, el Piggly Wiggly (store), el Thomason General Hospital (now University Medical Center), el Correlón de la Bowie (sport grounds behind the old Bowie High School), Salas Grocery de la Park Street, el Cashway, Safeway stores, Gunning

The Sacred Heart Church.

Casteel Drugs; el Ascarate Lake; el Bronco theatre; Cinema Park drive-in; Woolworth; el Burger Boy; ACME Laundry; el Hacienda Restaurant; el Colón, el Crawford; el Palace; el Calzetín; el Allanay; el State; el Plaza Theatre: el Border Tobacco; el Western Auto; la White House; McKinney shoe store downtown; el Liberty Hall; el Armijo Center; Sacred Heart Church; MECHA (Chicano Movement organization at UTEP started in the 1970s); El Pujido (where stabbings created a moaning cry); Weaver Scopes; Dr. Furigochi (a Japanese American doctor who deserves our thanks and greatest respect and admiration for his kind and generosity in helping the barrio people over and beyond the call of duty); Father Rahm; Chico's Tacos; el Oasis Restaurant en la Pershing; el Pershing Theater, el Coliseo (coliseum); el Chamizal; Raymond Tellez (first Mexican American mayor of El Paso, Texas, and ambassador under John F. Kennedy to Costa Rica); el Whoos Club, jam session dancing;

Chico's Tacos; el Washington Park; los Night Dreamers (band); el Leo's Finer Foods, opened in 1946; el Concordia; Fort Bliss; John Wesley Hardin (pioneer outlaw who killed more than forty men and later studied law during his nineteen years in prison); la montaña Franklin; los Curanderos del barrio; el Hotel Dieu (hospital); Jake Erlich (tallest man in the world-stood at 8 feet 6 ½ inches); el College of Mine (later Texas Western College, now the University of Texas at El Paso/UTEP); Cleofas Calleros (cofounder of the El Paso County Historical Society who coordinated the construction of the road up to Cristo Rey); el famoso Sun Bowl; los cachuchones; la Migra (border patrol and their infamous green hats).

Mexican American Acculturation into Mainstream United States— Its Dilemmas and Implications

In an article by Knight, Cota, and Bernal (1993), they state that the Mexican American children acquire the values transmitted to them by their mothers and that, in turn, makes them conform to their own culture and customs, emphasizing close family ties. It has been seen that Mexican families are very close and loyal members. As Valdés (1996) observes, some families he stated, for these families, prestige, intellectual achievement, and even wealth were less important than morality and family loyalty. Gloria Castor claims that

> the American Dream is the ultimate dream come true for many neighboring countries. Mexican-Americans become acculturated into the American culture. As the generations of the Mexican-Americans grow in the United States, the connection to the motherland (Mexico), its language, culture, and beliefs, is diminished….As time goes by, Mexican-American families slowly change their identity becoming more and more Americanized. Therefore, Mexican-American families, and teachers of these families should keep the culture alive for their children so it won't be lost forever…Many Mexican-Americans today don't see themselves connected to Mexican. Some have no relatives in Mexico and don't have the privilege of living near or going to visit the country, making them unfamiliar to their own

roots. Others feel a sense of embarrassment if the people around them identify them as a Mexican.

"I always possessed this horrid feeling of inadequacy for not being white. I had decided, since an early age that I would "fit in" (Sosa, M. 1999)…"It is important for Mexican-Americans to accept the fact that they are a unique group at a crossroads" (Mendoza, J. I., 1994) Cultural adaptation refers to the outcome in which individuals modify their cognitions, behaviors, and interpretations of behaviors to match the new cultural environment better. The fact of wanting to "fit in" leads to modification of identity… According to Perez and Padilla, if children immigrate at a very early age and if parents do not reinforce the home culture, children will experience an eventual loss of part or all of the home language. In turn, these children acquire accumulated knowledge of American culture and language through the school and peers…As much as we may try to become part of the mainstream, there will always be someone or some event that will remind us of who we are and where we came from; it is usually just enough to cause most of us to stop and remember our heritage. Mexican-Americans need to remember that the teaching of the mother language and culture start at home…Mexican-Americans living in the border have an advantage to a close relation with their motherland. Allowing them to have a better link to their heritage and culture. But it is believed that they have a culture of their own. According to Heyman, J.M. (2001), the Mexican-American people who live along the border have changed identities, and exchanged ideas and resources to simultaneously change and blend their cultures…

making this a border culture…Alvarez, R., states that when Mexican-Americans assimilate into the culture, they never truly lose their Mexican identity. Many of them in later life re-identify with Mexico and with being Mexican. "Although home culture diminishes across generations, it does not disappear completely" (Schultz, P.W.).

Taxonomy of Cultural Terms

Here is a summary of the various groups of people now numbered as descendents of the Spanish and Mexican peoples. This comes from soc.culture. mexican.ucla.edu70:

Spanish People

This term is used frequently in the United States to refer indiscriminately to any person that speaks Spanish. As such, it is imprecise and often inappropriate in that it includes people from more than two dozen countries, spanning all of the American continent, the Caribbean and Spain. The term does apply specifically, however, as the proper name for the native people of Spain, and for this reason it is as incorrect to use it to refer to any and all Spanish-speakers as the term "English" would be to refer to citizens of New Zealand, Australia or the United States.

Hispanics

This term is often used to refer collectively to all Spanish-speakers. However, it specifically connotes a lineage or cultural heritage related to Spain. As millions of people who speak Spanish are not of true Spanish descent (e.g., native Americans), and millions more live in Latin America yet do not speak Spanish or claim Spanish heritage (e.g., Brazilians) this term is incorrect as a collective name for all Spanish speakers, and may actually be cause for offense.

Latino

The term is used to refer to people originating from, or having a heritage related to, Latin America, in recognition of the fact that this set of people is actually a superset of many nationalities. Since the term "Latin" comes into use as the least common denominator for all peoples of Latin America in recognition of the fact that some romance language (Spanish, Portuguese, and French) is the native tongue of the majority of Latin Americans, this term is widely accepted by most. However, the term is not appropriate for the millions of native Americans who inhabit the region.

Mexican

Specifically, the nationality of the inhabitants of Mexico. Therefore, the term is used appropriately for Mexican citizens, who visit or work in the United States, but it is insufficient to designate those people who are citizens of the United States (they were born in the US or are naturalized citizens of the US) who are of Mexican ancestry.

Mexican American

It is important to explain why (some) people feel it is important to make a distinction. US citizens who are troubled by this often point out that most immigrants do not distinguish themselves by point of origin first, (i.e., German American), but simply as "Americans" (another troublesome term, but we won't get detoured by that here). Here are some reasons why many US citizens of Mexican extraction feel that it is important to make the distinction:

"Not Americans" by choice—a scant 150 years ago, approximately 50% of what was then Mexico was appropriated by the US as spoils of war, and in a series of land "sales" that were coerced capitalizing on the US victory in that war and Mexico's weak political and economic status. A sizable number of Mexican citizens became citizens of the United States from one day to the next as a result, and the treaty declaring the peace between the two countries recognized the rights of such people to their private properties (as deeded by Mexican or Spanish colonial authorities), their own religion (Roman Catholicism) and the right to speak and receive education in their own tongue (for the majority, Spanish) [refer to the text of the treaty of Guadalupe-Hidalgo]. Therefore, the descendants of this population continue to press for such rights, and many hold that theirs is a colonized land and people in view of the fact that their territory and population was taken over by military force.

Mexicans first, "Americans" second?—Another and more numerous class of US citizens of Mexican extraction are either descendants of, or are themselves, people who conceive of themselves as temporarily displaced from Mexico by economic circumstances. As opposed to the waves of European migrants who willingly left their countries due to class and religious discrimination, and sought to make their lives anew in the "new world" and never to return to the "old land," these displaced Mexicans typically maintain strong family ties in Mexico (by visiting periodically, and by investing their incomes in homes or kin in Mexico), and usually intend to return to Mexico provided they can become economically secured. Therefore these people maintain and nurture their children in their language, religion, and customs.

However, there is great tension within this population between those of Mexican birth who conceive of themselves as temporary guests in the US, and their descendants who are born in the US, are acculturated with the norms of broader US society in public schools, and are not motivated by the same ties that bind a migrant generation of Mexicans. This creates a classic "niche" of descendants of immigrants who are full-fledged US citizens, but who typically do not have access to all the rights and privileges of citizenship because of the strong cultural identity imbued in them by their upbringing and the discriminatory reaction of the majority population against a non-assimilated and easily identified subclass. This group of people feels a great need to distinguish itself from both its US milieu and its Mexican "Mother Culture," which does not typically welcome or accept "prodigals." This is truly a unique set of people, therefore, in that it endures both strong ties and strong discrimination from both US and Mexican mainstream parent cultures. The result has been the creation of a remarkable new culture that needs its own name and identity.

"Mexican American" is commonly used to recognize US citizens who are descendants of Mexicans, following the pattern sometimes used to identify the extraction of other ethnic Americans (e.g., "African American"). This term is acceptable to many Mexican descendants, but for those who do not identify with a Mexican heritage, but rather with a Spanish heritage, it is unacceptable (cf., "Hispano" following). Also, for those who do not view themselves as "Americans" by choice, this term is problematic, and for others the implication that the identity of the bearer is unresolved, or in limbo, between two antipodal influences, belies their self-concept as a blend that supersedes its origins and is stronger, richer and more dynamic than either of its cultural roots.

Hispano

This term is preferred by that subpopulation, located primarily in the US southwest, who identify with the Spanish settlers of the area, and not with the Mexican settlers (specifically, the Creole Spanish-Native American race). There is in fact an important number of these people located along the Rio Grande Valley of New Mexico and in the northern Sangre de Cristo mountain range of the same state. This group has been traditionally a very closed and conservative one, and recent evidence provides important explanations for this: they seem to be descendants of persecuted Jews who fled Spain during the 16th and 17th centuries and sought refuge in what were then the farthest reaches of the known world. They survived by minimizing their contact with outsiders and by hiding or disguising their religious and cultural identities as much as possible. Historical researchers call them "cryptic Jews."

Chicano

A relatively recent term that has been appropriated by many Mexican descendants as unique and therefore reflective of their unique culture, though its first usage seems to have been discriminatory. The most likely source of the word is traced to the 1930 and 40s period, when poor, rural Mexicans, often native Americans, were imported to the US to provide cheap field labor, under an agreement of the governments both countries. The term seems to have come into first use in the fields of California in derision of the inability of native Nahuatl speakers from Morelos state to refer to themselves as "Mexicanos," and instead spoke of themselves as "Mesheecanos," in accordance with the pronunciation rules of their language. An equivocal factor is that in vulgar Spanish it is common for Mexicans to use the "CH" conjunction in place of certain consonants in order to create a term of endearment. Whatever its origin, it was at first insulting to be identified by this name. The term was appropriated by Mexican American activists who took part in the Brown Power movement of the '60s and '70s in the US southwest, and has now come into widespread usage. Among more "assimilated" Mexican Americans, the term still retains an unsavory connotation, particularly because it is preferred by political activists and by those who seek to create a new and fresh identity for their culture rather than to subsume it blandly under the guise of any mainstream culture.

The next article, in my way of thinking, is how discrimination can be ended.

How to Put an End Forever to All Discrimination

This is an article in *El Paso Times* on March 19, 2002, "Drawing Race-Based Lines Is Problematic," by Maj. John Manza. Maj. Manza was a U.S. Marine stationed at Fort Bliss when he wrote about this experience.

My wife was at the Fort Bliss Hospital recently when she faced the inevitable bureaucratic question from a medical clerk: "What racial or ethnic group do you belong to?" Then, seeing my wife's olive-colored skin, he continued, "Should I list you as Hispanic?" My wife replied that she is not Hispanic, rather that she is Italian.

The clerk scanned his form for a suitable match, but was stumped. Finally, in desperation the clerk decided to check the box listed as "other."

My wife's experience says a lot about the problem of racial and ethnic classification. Such race-based classifications are irrelevant, clearly subjective, and morally indefensible.

Unfortunately, our government classifies the races and promotes the differences among them. One example is the state-sponsored recognition of selected ethnic groups through race-based awareness celebrations and heritage months. The U.S. government recognizes four such occasions: Black History, Hispanic Heritage, Asian-Pacific

Heritage, and Native American Heritage months. The government defends these celebrations as necessary to recognize the contributions of minorities and "people of color."

Determining status by skin color is highly problematic. Just look at the methods that the U.S. government employs to define "Hispanics." They are identified by the geographic area of the world their ancestors came from, the language they speak and by the color of their skin. The geographic list includes Mexico, Puerto Rico, Cuba, Central and South America and Spain. Government Web sites state there is a need to break out the Hispanic population because, unlike the "Caucasian/White" majority, they are prone to discrimination because they have darker skin color and speak Spanish.

This is foolish when one considers that the immigrant from Sicily or Greece, who is as dark skinned as many "people of color," is listed as White/Caucasian. Why? Because of arbitrary geographic boundaries we have drawn to define races.

The deeper one looks, the more absurd the policy becomes. There are millions of people in Argentina and Chile who are of German descent. Many have light complexions, blond hair and blue eyes, but they come from South America. Are they Hispanic? Many of those who emigrate from Argentina or Chile do not consider themselves Hispanic and list themselves instead as Caucasian.

And what about those from the Indian subcontinent and from the Middle East? Are they people of color? Should we care?

Many people point out that some groups have been discriminated against and therefore deserve special recognition. Where, then, is Jewish History Month? Have not Jews suffered enormous discrimination and even faced racial extermination?

I say it is time to stop classifying Americans according to race. We are not celebrating diversity when we lump people together into racial groups. Our people come in many shades, speak many languages, and believe in many religions. Our strength is our ability to bring these diverse groups together. Yes, we can be proud of our diverse ethnic heritage, but we must first be Americans.

Perhaps the hospital clerk was right. We Americans don't fit into neat racial groups. Maybe we should all just check the "other" block.

The Barrio Witch Doctors
—"Los Curanderos"

"Los curanderos" (faith healers); "parteras" (midwives); "hueseros" (bonesetters), also called "sobadores" (massagers or therapists); herbalists; and "mal de ojo" (evil eye); "leer las barajas" (card reading); and "leer las palmas de la manos" (palm reading) were an overpowering part of daily life in South El Paso. People in the barrio sought the services of healers and unlicensed practitioners before securing medical attention at the hands of professional doctors. These healers were accessible and easier to locate, especially in times of emergencies. Their mission was to bring quick comfort and mythical religious assurance to people in their daily existence.

The barrio people rarely questioned the credentials or backgrounds of healers. They dared not upset their self-proclaimed credibility by confronting them with questions concerning their medical practices or methods. That was considered taboo. No one questioned their integrity or their knowledge of the physical and spiritual implications of the healing process. Similarly, card readers, palm readers, and the herbalists, las parteras, the bonesetters, the massagers, and the curanderos—all of these healers—enjoyed virtually total freedom and absolute power over the psyches of the people. Their medieval practices and their superior wisdom—whether based on myth or fable, from an educational background or not—were a highly sought after form of remedy to the ailments and their cost for services rendered was within the means of people. The curanderos were compassionate, charismatic, and for the most part, sympathetic to the people's maladies.

Adeline Short Dinger writes about the early days in Brownsville, Texas, and describes some aspects of the mythical curative powers of the curanderos and their employment of medicinal herbs, plants, and their oftentimes crude methods of dealing with the supernatural:

> Within the memory of present-day survivors of the early days in Brownsville, there was a time when curanderos, the healers or witch doctors who were believed to possess curative powers, watched closely by the bedside of one whose life was ebbing. If all restorative means failed, the curandero must have at hand a supply of sky rockets to be shot off the instant the patient expired. The explosion of the rocket served a dual purpose, for in addition to frightening the evil spirits who inevitably waited hopefully for the departing, the soaring rocket acted as a guide to the soul, leading it upward on its journey to the spirit-realm. Rockets were shot at intervals proceeding the time of burial and were a necessary accompaniment to the funeral cortege. No inconsistency was felt in adapting the usages of the church to the practices of the curanderos. In the case of a young girl, even a very small child, it was a common practice to dress the corpse in robes modeled after the blue drapings of the Virgin of Guadalupe before the mourners set out upon the rocket-punctuated journey to the grave.
>
> Belief in the power of curanderos is firmly implanted in the minds of many of the modern Latin population, and has colored the thinking of many native residents who have no Latin antecedents. One explanation lies in the discovery that in many witch doctor practices there is a germ of scientific truth; the actual curative properties of many commonly used medicinal herbs and plants. Lore concerning the use of these common

things was handed down from antiquity, often a closely guarded secret. The present day curandero profits by the credulity of his clientele, dispensing the potions he compounds from familiar herbs (usually purchased from a wholesale distributor) along with the accompanying "magic" ritual which is supposed to produce the desired result.

The Catholic Church sanctioned, to some extent, the curanderos' practice because of its Catholic-based faith despite its mixture of mystical-spiritual foundations but the professional medical society at large preferred not to intervene. In some fateful cases, however, disastrous results could have been prevented had professional doctors intervened. Impoverishment, the Mexican culture and its evolutionary history dating back centuries was usually at the heart of all the unfortunate situations.

Curanderismo and its impact upon modern research and investigation are lengthy. Its origins can be traced back to the early civilizations of the old world and the newer ones of the Spaniards in the fifteenth century. The following study by Mark Hoenig, associate director of Centro de la Familia de Utah (formerly IHRD), Salt Lake City, Utah, 1993, gives some important historical data and academic insight which may give greater meaning to the practice of curanderismo in relationship to present day matters of health:

Every society develops a medical system by which illness is conceptualized and the well-being of the community is maintained. The scientific model, as defined in the West, sometimes conflicts with the medical models of other cultures when practitioners of the former engage in efforts to address a particular health problem.

In such cases, the intentions of medical health providers may be good, and their methods of cure may be effective, but providers of an unfamiliar medical system will often meet resistance when trying to introduce new methods to a targeted population. The indigenous medical system of Latin America, curanderismo, is a case in point. Founded on principles contrary to those of modern medicine (but with similar origins), curanderismo is an important form of healing in many communities in the United States. This should come as no surprise; immigration of Mexican nationals into the United States includes an infusion of cultural traits as well as people. As such, the existence of curanderismo has been documented by Scheper-Hughes, & Steward (1983) and Perrone & Stockel (1984) in New Mexico; by Kay (1981) in Arizona; by Clark (1959) and Roberts & Lee (1980) in California; and by Quesada & Heller (1977) in Texas. These studies, however, do not all suggest that curanderismo is a permanent or unchanging system by which matters of health are addressed? Scheper-Hughes and Steward (1983), for example, point out that although curanderismo does exist in northern New Mexico in some form, "time and acculturation seem to have greatly eroded the belief in and practice of curanderismo." Others have noted the diminishing importance of curanderismo as alter natives to modern psychotherapy. This is significant, for many (see Kiev, 1968; Torrey, 1972; and Arenas, Cross, and Willard, 1980) claim that its greatest strengths, and hence its continuance as a viable medical alternative, lie in its ability to adequately address illnesses of non-somatic origin. In addition to "Mexican folk psychiatry" (Kiev, 1968) definitions of curanderismo have included traditional folk medical beliefs and practices; ritualistic acts traditionally considered to have favorable effects on health; and the use of folk medical curers (Aguirre, 1978). However defined, curanderismo is a collection of traits from various medical traditional Aztec, Spanish, and modern Western medicine. Indigenous Spanish healing can be traced to the time of the Spanish conquest of the Americas in the 15th century. They brought with them their medical knowledge, which was based largely on classical Greek and Roman medicine with its emphasis on humoral pathology, and incorporated elements of the medical system already being practiced in the new world. Curanderismo also has a heavy infusion of Catholicism, as can be seen in Rubel's (1960) classic description of Mexican curing rituals in which a victim of susto (medical fright) is laid down with arms outstretched as in a cross and prayers recited over him. Curanderos, however, are not regarded as the equivalent to the Catholic clergy. Their major attribute, according to Kiev (1968), is their religiosity, but the two represent different conceptual models. Another premise of curanderismo that differs from that of scientific medicine is the belief that the patient is regarded as an innocent victim, subject to forces not always within his or her control. Within modern medicine is the belief that a person assumes responsibility for both his and her own well-being and poor health, that is, 'at fault' if illness is incurred…in spite of these differences, curanderismo is recognized as a comprehensive form of medical care. It addresses the physical as well as emotional needs of its adherents. However, studies of Curanderismo focus on the non-somatic aspects of its abilities to cure, and this model is always included in studies that determine the cultural barriers of Mexican-Americans to receiving health care."

The curanderos also performed the labor of purging out malignancies such as the "empachado" (constipation, glutted or fed to satiety, sick person) by rubbing lard or oil throughout the person's body and massaging with extreme care the affected areas of pain, while at times reciting incantations. When the empachado was cleared of his misfortune or his health completely restored, he would then be freed from evil spirits that were blamed for being the perpetrators of illness. If all home remedies failed, the patient was forced to seek the aid of the curandero; not an ordinary herb doctor but a healer skilled in the ritualistic practices of dispelling evil. The most commonly described method of treatment involves the use of a cross made of ashes upon the floor. The patient must lie, face downward and arms outstretched, upon this cross.

The healer recites the usual prayers and incantations while making sweeping motions, in the form of a cross, with a broom over the prostrate form of the afflicted one, thus sweeping away the evil spell. After due ceremony, sometimes lasting for two hours, the cure was pronounced effected and the patient was released.

Probably the most widely spread superstitious belief is the commonly accepted idea of mal de ojo, or the evil eye. This spell is not always cast at the will of the evildoer, but may be the result of his admiring regard or of a covetous glance, without any harmful intent. It was considered an offense for one to admire a baby or to ask its name without first touching some part of its body.

The belief, said to be of Indian origin, still prevails that evil in the eye may convey paralysis or some other destructive malady to any part of the body under regard. The standard home treatment for mal de ojo is the rubbing of an egg over the fevered brow of the patient. Continued rubbing is said to draw out the evil, reducing the high temperature to such extent that the heat absorbed often coagulates the white of the egg. Sometimes an egg is broken and placed in a saucer under the bed of the patient. If an 'eye' forms about the yoke of the egg, observers may know that the spell has been removed.

The curanderos were said to do a profitable business in the sale of magic potions or charms, which are supposed to counteract the spell of the evil eye or the "put-upon" curse. The curse is different from the mal de ojo in that it involves a deliberate, willful act. It may be mental, or it may be administered in physical form, such as a powder inserted into a cigarette or dissolved in a drink. Only a skilled curandero was able to prepare such a potion. In one legendary story of the magical spells of the potion, an unfortunate man was so ugly that the girl of whom he was enamored spurned his advances. When ordinary methods of wooing failed, he resorted to his cunning in the mixing of magic herbs. When the powder was prepared, he enlisted the aid of a friend who poured it into the coffee of his adored one. Success was immediate. The girl fell madly in love with her homely suitor, and they were married within two weeks.

The Medicinal Application of Indian Herbs

Here is an article I've had for several years; it all fits with what I remember from my childhood:

> In conjunction with the curanderos, life without the traditional folk medicine to find cure for health ailments like the common cold or flu was impossible. Herbs have always had a pleasant and important existence in the Mexican home. For instance, old remedies normally contained such herbs as "hierba Buena" (Peppermint leaves) boiled in water sweetened to one's own taste to calm children's stomach cramps, and "Té de Canela" (Tea from Cinnamon sticks) plain or sweetened also or combined with a doze of Tequila for sore throats, flu colds, and upset stomachs. Children or young people on rare occasions were permitted to sip tequila in an herbal mixture. The older generation conveniently justified their Tequila mixtures with herbs to rid of health problems on a more common and acceptable basis. The list of herbs is varied and quite extensive. They were uniquely applied to most every infirmity known to the people from the Barrio. Consider the following herbs and their medicinal value:
>
> El ajo, or garlic, basic ingredient and seasoning of many Mexican dishes, is believed to possess valuable curative qualities. The tender buds,

crushed in the molcajete, or mortar and mixed with brown sugar or added to thick sugar syrup, furnish a potent remedy for whooping cough or any persistent couch. Liberal use of garlic in the diet is said to prevent scurvy. A tea or infusion of the garlic bulb is prescribed for daily use in the treatment of stomach ulcers, liver and kidney disorders, and even as means of reducing high blood pressure. Crushed garlic is also applied to relieve pain resulting from the sting of the Alacrán or poisonous scorpion.

The cebolla, or onion, has similar uses and is recommended beside as a poultice for burns. Mixed with hot vinegar it is used as a chest compress for croup or pneumonia.

Cominos, or cumin seed, another common seasoning, is a versatile remedio. An infusion of the seed is given to newborn babies for colic or other digestive disturbances, also for teething ills. The same remedy is used as eyewash in treatment of pinkeye or inflamed lids.

Buena mujer is the poetic name for the common nightshade. The fruit of this plant, prepared for local application, is believed to be beneficial in treating cataract of the eye. An infusion of the root is used for abdominal pain. A woman can determine the sex of her child by eating portions of this plant. The pounded berries may be added to milk to hasten curdling in the preparation of queso, a hard white cheese.

Cachane, (heart-leaf) is said to facilitate conception.

Seeds of the <u>calabaza</u>, or small Mexican pumpkin, highly favored when toasted and pulverized as an ingredient of mole and other native sauces, are also credited with curative power in cases of tapeworm and kidney and intestinal inflammation

<u>Conejo</u> is the descriptive name given to the wild larkspur, the blossoms of which are thought to resemble a long-eared rabbit. An infusion of this plant used as a cathartic is said to relieve rheumatism and spastic paralysis.

Tea brewed from the common dandelion, <u>diente de león,</u> is given as a tonic for dyspepsia and for liver and kidney disorders.

Extract of the leaves of the <u>huele de noche</u>, or night-blooming jasmine, is used for convulsions, spasms, and epilepsy.

<u>Cenizo</u>, the barometer bush whose purplish blossoms bring promise of rain, is valued for medicinal uses. An infusion of the blossoms serves as a cough remedy.

Leaves, twigs, and bark soaked in water which is added to the bath, are said to allay weariness, renew strength, and even relieve suffering due to tuberculosis.

Bark of <u>amargosa,</u> or goat brush, contains a substance which, in infusion, is used as a substitute for quinine for malarial chills. It is said, also, to relieve dysentery and colic.

Less widely known is the canchalagua, or quinine weed. The infusion of this plant is mixed with whiskey as a remedy for influenza.

Barbas de chiva, old man's beard, the pest of Valley fruit groves, serves a useful purpose as a poultice for fresh sores. As a cosmetic an infusion of the flowers is applied for removing freckles. The powdered root is a diuretic. The root of the althea, also, is used as a diuretic, and the powder, mixed with lard, is applied for skin eruptions.

Flowers of the dill, or agrios, are used in infusion, for colic or for prolonged hiccups.

The seeds of the amapola, or wild poppy, have well-known soporific effect in cases of insomnia.

Skins of the granada, small fruit of the pomegranate shrub frequently used for hedges, or the outer parings of the root, are boiled to produce a nauseous broth recommended for the treatment of internal cancer. This medicine was prepared by a maid of Indian origin and offered to her mistress, who was dreading a series of radium treatments. After satisfying herself through scientific research that the pomegranate had been in medicinal use among ancient Romans, Greeks, and Egyptians, the patient consented to the dosage. Results were astoundingly successful.

Cancer, a curly-leafed grey-green weed bearing tiny scarlet blossoms grows profusely over the desert country and is even cultivated in the gardens of herb healers, is said to furnish, in poultices, a most effective remedy for abscessed sores or carbuncles and for the removal of grano or tumor.

Ruda, or rue, is grown as a specific for earache.

Manzanilla, the ornamental flowering shrub, is used in a remedy for dropsy and stomach disorders. The soft, pulpy leaves of la bruja (a succulent air-plant, the leaves of which suspended in the air, send out tiny sprouts) are split and placed cut side down over the stomach of an infant to relieve colic pain.

Amor seco, a small prolific weed with star-shaped yellow blossoms, is commonly used in a strong brew for the dreaded dysentery of infants, and the leaves are pressed over the gums to relieve the pain of teething.

Drago, a shrub that produces the tiny nut providing food for the native "white-winged" pigeons, is useful to man, also. The pulpy wood yields a soapy substance highly esteemed for cleaning the teeth and washing the hair. Tradition says that drago is the secret of the fine teeth and luxuriant hair commonly noticed in certain localities.

The Consequential Marriage of the Indian and the Spaniard Gives Birth to the Mexican

One of my grandmothers was about 50 percent Apache. She was slightly smaller than the average women of today. She was an expert cook, a serious disciplinarian, hardworking, caring, close-knitted, and hopeful that her descendents to have better things in life. She was married to a Mexican who had ridden with Pancho Villa. He was an agricultural expert. He knew how to work the dry land of early El Paso when it was part of the region now known as Juarez, Mexico.

During that time my grandmother lived, her own people, the Apache people, would attack settlers like her husband and their families. The Indians came down from the Franklin Mountains and stole cattle, horses, sheep, and young women. They also sought the merciless death of males and all who stood in their way. Their attacks were continuous and devastated whole families when these occurred. That was a difficult time for my Apache grandma, and one that caused her to form deep feelings against her own blood people. We can only imagine the turmoil in her life.

Decades later, as we look for answers to serious questions about discrimination, it is enlightening to begin with our roots. Michael Coe, in his book *America's First Civilization*, shows us how two different races can come together: the first Native Americans and the first Spaniards who found their way into the New World.

Hundreds of years ago, the only people who lived in the New World were the Native Americans. With time, the Spanish conquistadors began making their way into these unexplored lands.

The Spanish people had an experience like no other. They not only stepped into unfamiliar territory but were introduced to a different type of people whom they had never met or seen before. They had no idea that the natives even existed. Two different races met for the first time. It would not be long before the two cultures with their traditions and languages would undergo major changes that would change history forever. The two races were both set in their ways. They were stubborn and conflicts became a way of life. Learning to compromise and accept each other came slowly, and as a result, many people perished. The Spanish people were prepared to use whatever methods were available to them in order to ensure that all their efforts would not be in vain. Many Spanish men married and fathered children of Indian women and another race was soon created. These offspring came to be known as Mexicans. The Mexican people are the descendents of the first Native Americans and the first Spaniards who found their way into the New World.

William H. Prescott, perhaps the most famous historian of ancient Americans and the continent they inhabited long before the arrival of the Spanish conquistadors, has written a most prolific and detailed account of the civilizations which gave way to the Mexican culture of today:

> Midway across the continent, somewhat nearer the Pacific than the Atlantic Ocean, at an elevation of nearly seven thousand five hundred feet, is the celebrated Valley of Mexico. It is of an oval form, about sixty-seven leagues in circumference, and is encompassed by a towering rampart of porphyritic rock, which nature seems to have provided, though ineffectually, to protect it from invasion.
>
> The soil, once carpeted with a beautiful verdure, and thickly sprinkled with stately trees, is often bare, and, in many places, white with the incrustation of salts, caused by the draining of the waters. Five lakes are spread over the Valley,

occupying one tenth of its surface. On the opposite borders of the largest of these basins, much shrunk in its dimensions since the days of the Aztecs, stood the cities of Mexico and Tezcuco, the capitals of the two most potent and flourishing states of Anahuac, whose history, with that of the mysterious races that preceded them in the country, exhibits some of the nearest approaches to civilization to be met with anciently on the North American continent.

Of these races the most conspicuous were the Toltecs. Advancing from a northerly direction, but from what region is uncertain, they entered the territory of Anahuac, probably before the close of the seventh century…the Toltecs were well instructed in agriculture, and many of the most useful mechanic arts; were nice workers of metals; invented the complex arrangement of time adopted by the Aztecs; and, in short, were the true fountains of the civilization which distinguished this part of the continent in later times. They established their capital at Tula, north of the Mexican Valley, and the remains of extensive buildings were to be discerned there at the time of the Conquest.

The noble ruins of religious and other edifices, still to be seen in various parts of New Spain, are referred to this people, whose name, Toltec, has passed into a synonym for architect. Their shadowy history reminds us of those primitive races, who preceded the ancient Egyptians in the march of civilization; fragments of whose monuments, as they are seen at this day, incorporated with the buildings of the Egyptians themselves, give to these latter the appearance of almost modern construction.

After a period of four centuries, the Toltecs, who had extended their sway over the remotest borders of Anahuac, having been greatly reduced, it is said, by famine, pestilence, and unsuccessful wars, disappeared from the land as silently and mysteriously as they had entered it... After the lapse of another hundred years, a numerous and rude tribe, called the Chichemecs entered the deserted country from the regions of the far North-west. They were speedily followed by other races, of higher civilization, perhaps of the same family with the Toltecs, whose language they appear to have spoken. The most noted of these were the Aztecs, or Mexicans, and the Acolhuans. The latter, known in later times by the name of Tezcucans, from their capital, Tezcuco, on the eastern border of the Mexican lake, were peculiarly fitted, by their comparatively mild religion and manners, for receiving the tincture of civilization which could be derived from the few Toltecs that still remained in the country. This, in turn, they communicated to the barbarous Chichemecs, a large portion of whom became amalgamated with the new settlers as one nation.

The Mexicans, with whom our history is principally concerned, came also, as we have seen, from the remote regions of the north, the populous hive of nations in the New World, as it has been in the Old. They arrived on the borders of Anahuac towards the beginning of the thirteenth century, sometime after the occupation of the land by the kindred races. For a long time they did not establish themselves in any permanent residence; but continued shifting their quarters to different parts of the Mexican Valley, enduring all the casualties and hardships of a migratory life. On one occasion, they were enslaved by a more powerful tribe; but their ferocity soon made them formidable to their masters. After a series of wanderings and adventures, which need not shrink from comparison with the most extravagant legends of the heroic ages of antiquity, they at length halted on the south-western borders of the principal lake, in the year 1325. They there beheld, perched on the stem of a prickly pear, which shot out from crevice of a rock that was washed by the waves, a royal eagle of extraordinary size and beauty, with a serpent in his talons, and his broad wings open to the rising sun. They hailed the auspicious omen, announced by an oracle as indicating the site of their future city, and laid its foundations by sinking piles into the shallows; for the low marshes were half buried under water. On these they erected their light fabrics of reeds and rushes; and sought a precarious subsistence from fishing, and from the wild fowl which frequented the waters, as well as from the cultivation of such simple vegetables as they could rise on their floating gardens. The place was called Tenochtitlan, in token of its miraculous origin, though only known to Europeans by its other name Mexico, derived from their war god, Mexitli. The legend of its foundation is still further commemorated by the device of the eagle and the cactus, which form the arms of the modern Mexican republic. Such were the humble beginnings of the Venice of the Western World.

The Socio-Culture of Love and Power in the Mexican Family

It is easier to understand today after we have examined the past. Most of us have received information about our ancestors from our parents and grandparents. Our folk's related stories and histories intended to help us understand and appreciate our cultural heritage. In the process, we also were finding out who we are as a people and as individuals. This search for our identity continues. R. Diaz-Guerrero has some interesting comments in his book *Psychology of the Mexican* as does Guadalupe Valdés in *Con Respeto*. We'll start with Mr. Diaz-Guerrero:

> Early in the sixteenth century, a few hundred Spaniards conquered a land inhabited, according to historians, by eight million Indians. Its whole sociocultural historical background is based upon the union of a conqueror—the powerful, the male, the Spaniard—and the conquered—the female, the subjugated, the Indian. For a period of time it was believed that Indians had no souls but that children born to Spaniards and Indian women had them. I have jokingly remarked that it was undoubtedly a fervent religious zeal that led these few hundred Spaniards to put souls into the bodies of Indian women; this zeal created modern Mexico with its almost entirely mestizo *Webster's New Collegiate Dictionary*: "a person of mixed blood; specifically: a person of mixed European and American Indian ancestry" population.

Sometime, somehow, consciously or unconsciously, this relationship crystallized into a decision that seems to hold the key to most dealings both within the Mexican family and within the Mexican socio-culture. The decision was that all power was to be in the hands of the male and all love was to be in the hands of the female. Ever since, it appears, the male obtains the love of the female through a mythical mixture of power and love; any power the female acquires is by means of her loving behavior…in Mexican interactions power and love are almost never completely separated from each other. One might say that there is not a significant differentiation between these two patterns of interpersonal interaction in the Mexican socio-culture.

In the United States, where most people were confident that they were equal to anyone else, for a long time the system ideally treated them all equally (i.e., they all had equal rights under the law) but gave them different jobs in accordance with their cognitive ability and technical capacity. In Mexico, where all are theoretically equal as far as affect is concerned, power went to the loved ones. Thus in the Mexican socio-culture power is bestowed, traditionally, upon those you love: your nuclear family, the extended family, your relatives, friends, etc. The American socio-culture is the socio-culture of power, and power is the main element in decision making. Mexico, on the other hand, is still a socio-culture of love, and final decisions are made in terms more of affiliation than of power. It is within the warm network of affiliation that the Mexican grows into an interdependent, obedient individual. The Mexican socio-culture, then, is an affiliative and hierarchical culture. In effect, power is primarily in the hands of the father; the mother also has power in terms of love and respect; and the rest are assumed to obey…The two extremes of the age continuum, the elderly and the very young, hold the highest status in the society. They are given respect, power, and love. Let us recall what is said about babies in Mexico: they are called los reyes de la casa, "the kings of the household." The elderly, the grandparents, who traditionally hold power over ultimate decisions, share this status.

Guadalupe Valdés adds further insight:

> The relationship between mothers and their children cannot be understood without an examination of one of the most important notions guiding interaction between individuals in these families. This notion is respeto, a concept that goes much beyond the meaning of the English term respect.
>
> Respeto in its broadest sense is a set of attitudes toward individuals and/or the roles that they occupy. It is believed that certain roles demand or require particular types of behavior. Respeto, while important among strangers, is especially significant among members of the family. Having respeto for one's family involves functioning according to specific views about the nature of the roles filled by the various members of the family (e.g., husband, wife, son, brother). It also involves demonstrating personal regard for the individual who happens to occupy that role.
>
> Comments such as "La madre tiene que encargarse de la conducta de los hijos" (Mothers

have got to take responsibility for their children's behavior) and "Los hijos tienen que obedecer" (Children have to be obedient) reflect a set of rules that were accepted as governing the behavior of individuals occupying particular roles. Attitudes and expectations about roles served as a blueprint that guided the behavior of individuals as well as the response of other members of the family to their behavior.

The role of the father, for example, was seen to involve providing for his family as well as serving as an authority figure for his children. He was supposed to make sacrifices, work long hours, and ideally provide a good example for his sons. The role of the mother was seen to include managing the household in its broadest sense and raising the children to become good human beings.

The role of children was less well defined. However, as buenos hijos (good sons and daughters), they had an obligation to be considerate, obedient, and appreciative of their parents' efforts. As little children, they were not expected to contribute directly to the family in any large sense. However, they were expected, even at a very young age, not to behave in a manner that would result in more work for their parents. They were expected not to be selfish, to look after their siblings, and not to draw energy away from common family goals.

The view of the roles of father, mother, wife, and husband were traditional ones. There was little flexibility in the ways in which individuals could choose to live those roles. From very early on, children were socialized to accept certain definitions for these roles and to expect that they themselves would fill them in these ways. The ideal for an individual member of the family was for him or her to fill the role as expected and, in so doing, to personally earn respect (darse a respetar) due to that effort. Nevertheless, when a family member failed in key obligations that were part of the role he occupied, respeto was still owed by family members to the role itself.

Interactions between family members, then, were guided by respect for particular persons as well as respect for the obligations, rights, and privileges of the roles occupied by each individual. Older brothers, for example, had certain responsibilities to the family and to younger siblings, as well as certain privileges. Younger siblings were expected to respect their older siblings' authority and to understand the relationship between the privileges and obligations that were part of that role.

The Mexican Macho Man

Machismo and/or the super personality of the Mexican male has for generations been fantasized, romanticized, exploited, and heralded into a widespread phenomenon throughout Mexico. It has become the subject of folklore, song, dance, literature, and has now been portray by multiple artists in the motion picture industry and, to some extent, the stage. The famous Beach Boys have entertained and sung highly captivating music for decades related to the macho man. According to folklorist such as Vicente T. Mendoza, Ezequiel Martines, Samuel Ramos, Octavio Paz, Santiago Ramirez, Felipe Montemayor and others, the macho man in Mexico is typically characterized as one wearing a wide-brimmed sombrero, carrying a gun, riding a horse, boastful of his exploits, and continually subjecting women to "his nature, pleasure, and pride." Furthermore, the well-known writers above attest to the wide influence of this superhero, at times villain, dating back to early Spain when the conquistadors settled in Mexico and mercilessly "raped the women of the Aztecs." The coming together of the Spaniard and the Indian gave birth to the "mestizo" and/or the Mexican. Since then, the macho man has baffled writers, psychologists, historians, poets, and even folklorist to date. Much of the macho man folklore continues to resurrect the notorious Mexican general called Pancho Villa as if he is still alive.

Historically and something unfortunate to relate, the real macho man, or some of the Mexican husbands of times past and even today, has become a character associated with cruelty, violence, the continual punishment of women related to the consumption of alcohol. This male characteristic is still known to be applied in the continuous belittling, battering, and causing serious physical harm to his woman or wife and, in some cases, even to his own children too. He considers his cruel self-proclaimed principle as the last word in the family. There is no room for debate or questions against his extreme behavior.

The immediate and extended family have no say so and are quickly dismissed from getting involved into what the Mexican macho man considers to be personal matters beyond anybody else's control. His own rule of law cannot be challenged. The woman continues to be forced to undergo brutal acts of violence by the macho man who considers himself as the ultimate power in the family. He also prides himself in his skillful art of justification for his actions. He, however, oftentimes blames his actions upon society, due to the pressure of stagnation and routine and little or no salary advancement in the workplace. He places blame upon others in general, but not on his own self. His tends to employ vulgarity and other forms of ill manners to manage his familial affairs in and outside the home. Additionally, his lack of education and his typical poor family background causes him to become intellectually or spiritually disengaged in worth in his own community.

Once sober, he repents and regrets the harm he has caused on his own dedicated wife. She is seen as completely scared, defenseless, and secretly confiding her fight and trauma to people she can only trust. Even though she is the subject of trauma at the expense of her own husband, she will rarely contact law officials. Children witnessing unsightly bruises, blood, and disfigured faces expose them to incorrigible behavior at home that usually leads them into problems at school or even in the workplace later on.

They hid these happenings deep down in their own psyches. This may explain why so many children and teenagers become unruly and hard to deal with at an early age. Unaware of life at home, harsh disciplinary measures are often taken by school and law officials. They regularly are poor judges of family situation affecting children, teenagers and adolescents. It is of no consequence why so many jails and prison are overcrowded with individuals who have never had a decent home away from the brutal macho man influence.

Personally, this author witnessed the horrible damage a brother-in-law caused upon one of his sisters due to the consumption of alcohol. She was drenched in blood and her face was an awful sight to see. He offered her touching words to help her emotionally but to no avail. She was in deep pain, tearfully clutching her stomach, and carefully cleaning her face with a towel. The author could have beaten him up since he was smaller in stature, or called in law enforcers of law to get rid of this troublesome malady in the family. However, his own determination and his sister's unwillingness to seek more serious help from legal entities placed him in an undesirable position to not get involved. This unwelcomed battering or physical abuse by my brother-in-law against my sister was repeated periodically in the middle of the night for a number of years. His sister just took it in stride and forgave him somewhat for his actions. Her kindness and complete dedication to her family's welfare, the author thought, may have blinded and prevented her from seeming help through other social means or even from the standpoint of the law. Perhaps, her economic insecurity and a large family were considerable factors weighing heavily upon her shoulders and preventing her from availing of legal action.

The mental trauma and physical pain caused by those who engage in brutal acts against their own family members establishes a lack of trust, friendship, respect, and bonding that is essential for growth and prosperity in the realm of life in America. It also hampers and incapacitates to a great degree the pursuit of educational achievements and goals associated with the American Dream. The after effects of physical abuse are psychologically, mentally, and physically long-lasting. Brutal actions against loved ones are not easy to forget. They do not disappear naturally. They are always present in the psyches of those who have undergone trauma of this sort. Considering the nature of the effects of alcohol and related abuse, it affected this author in the most positive manner. He has never resorted to brutal force against his own wife in fifty years of marriage. The only times he ever laid his hands upon her, including his own children, were when she requested blessings. Especially, prior to her decision and willingness to undergo chemotherapy treatment for cancer at one point in the author's lifetime. Lastly, one of his sister's daughters said to this author, "I'm glad that idiot is dead!" To date, this niece has not forgiven her own father for his abusive actions and the pain he caused upon the family during her growing-up years.

El Rey

By Jose Alfredo Jimenez
Sung by: Vicente "Chente" Fernandez
And Artistically Translated by Ivan Estrella de los Angeles

Yo se bien que estoy afuera
Pero el dia en que yo me muera,
Se que tendras qua llorar

Llorar, llorar, llorar y llorar!

Diras que no me quisiste
Pero vas a estar muy triste, y asi te me vas a quedar.

Con dinero o sin dinero;
Hago siempre lo que quiero,
y mi palabra es la ley.

No tengo trono ni reina
Ni nadie que me comprenda,
Perso sigo siendo el Rey.

Una piedra en el camino
Me enseño que mi destino, era rodar y rodar

Despues me dijo un arriero
Que no hay que llegar primero
Pero hay que saber llegar!

Con dinero y sin dinero;
Hago siempre lo que quiero,
y mi palabra es la ley.

FÉLIX VALENZUELA

The King

I know well that I am an outsider but when I die,
Oh, I know you will cry
Cry, cry, cry, and cry!
You say that you never loved me
But you are going to be oh so sad,
That's the way it'll be
With, and without money,
I do what I please,
And my word is the law.
I don't have a throne nor a queen,
Nor even one to understand me,
Yet, I'm still the king.
A pebble in the road,
Showed me that my destiny, is to roll, and to roll
then the shepherd told me,

It's not about getting there first,
It's about knowing how to
Get there!
With and without money,
I do what I please,
And my word is the law.

Storytelling in the Barrio

Paulette Atencio says in her book *Cuentos from Long Ago*:

> Our ancestors have been telling stories to their children at least since 1598, when the first Spanish families settled along the Chama River in northern New Mexico. A four-hundred-year-old tradition began during that first harsh winter, when the warmth of the rustic hearths beckoned and warmed the settlers throughout their first winters.
>
> "Los cuentos" (the stories) are imbued with very strong dramatic and uplifting effects. The characters and situations are presented with much enthusiasm and vigor. Due to the romantic character of the Spanish language, many of the words or phrases used are poetic in nature and appeal to our emotions.
>
> My mother at heart was a prolific storyteller of tales such as "La Llorona," (a mournful ghost or weeping lady who cries over the loss of her children, whom she drowned after being spurned by her husband), "El Soldado Mocho," (the headless soldier whose head was blown off by a cannon during the Mexican Revolution) and "La Mano Negra" (the black hand who wanders alone from place to place without attachment to a complete physical body) and other supernatural apparitions. Neighborhood kids, along with our cousins, would gather in our little apartment to hear "los cuentos" (story telling) at its very best. My mom had a gift for psyching us out

and holding our attention for hours at a time. Her sincere belief in the supernatural was an outstanding psychological and spiritual trait throughout her life. She was by tradition a believer in ghosts, phantoms, the obscure, myths, and superstition. This was due in part to her illiterate upbringing and the lack of educational opportunities in Mexico. She attended school up to the third grade. Her stories of ghosts and other macabre tales maintained strong behavioral control over us. The unfolding of the terrifying implications of La Llorona, El Soldado Mocho, and La Mano Negra were situations in the Barrio none of us ever wanted to confront, especially La Llorona. Here is my mother's version of the famous La Llorona:

La Llorona

It was summertime and Doña Sofía's father had come back from Wyoming, where he worked as a sheepherder. He had saved money in order to fix up the old house where his family lived. The roof was in poor condition, and through the years, the rain, snow, and neglect had damaged the walls, ceiling, and floors. After the roof was fixed, the walls were plastered once again with mud and straw to reinforce the old adobe house. The flooring in one of the bedrooms was deteriorating and Doña Sofía's father decided to pour a cement floor.

When the work was finally completed, Doña Sofía's mother prepared supper and everyone ate outside. It was early in the evening and the entire family gathered around while Doña Sofía's father played the violin. It was customary for the neighbors to get together in the evening after long hours of hard work. The men would play horseshoes and the ladies would talk, laugh, and catch up on the gossip. The younger children would catch toritos (beetles) and butterflies. The older ones would jump from one side of the ditch to the other. Whoever fell into the ditch and got wet was the loser and the punishment was to go alone to Lillian's Orchard, an old vacant lot, and steal some purple plums and apples for all the children. It was considered a scary place.

Lillian's Orchard was deathly quiet, old, and dark. The birds never seemed to sing and the small creatures there were well hidden. Many of the trees were ugly looking, twisted, and took the form of threatening faces. This place gave everybody the creeps because so many horrible stories were told about it. In order to get there, one had to cross over a narrow and squeaky bridge that would swing back and forth. Doña Sofía told me that every so often at Lillian's Orchard, an old lady in a beautiful satin dress would try to snatch the children. Because she was so old and almost blind, everybody could outrun her. It would be safe to say that the entire community believed that it was La Llorona. All the children who had seen and heard her would come back running and crying louder than La Llorona herself. They all vowed obedience from that point on. This was the main reason why all the children stayed close to home and tried hard not to play the ditch game or fall in the water.

On this particular evening, everybody was having a wonderful time at Doña Sofía's house. Since they were not able to sleep on the freshly poured cement bedroom floor, mattresses were placed on the living room floor. The night was beautiful. The windows and doors were left open except for the screens on the windows and the screen door. The entire family could hear the crickets and the sound of the water from the ditch not far from the house. Finally, everybody fell asleep.

Doña Sofía remembers waking up and hearing someone crying. In a hurry she woke her parents. It was not long before the entire family was awake and listening. Doña Sofía's parents thought that maybe it was Tita, one of their neighbors. Her husband would drink moonshine, go crazy, come home, and beat up his wife. They all went outside but everything seemed peaceful around the neighborhood. Shortly afterward, one by one, all the neighbors started coming out of their houses. They also wondered who was crying and why.

At this point, Doña Sofía took my hand and held it while she continued her story. She described the shrieking cries as very painful and heartbreaking. The whines would penetrate right through the heart and soul of any human. In fact, it was enough to make one's hair stand up and for one to get goose bumps. According to Doña Sofía, it was not long before they all saw a figure running down the main dirt road. It called out, "Don't be afraid, I'm your local priest, Salomón Roybal." He was very scared and out of breath. He was letting everybody know that a demon in the form of La Llorona was roaming the streets looking for her lost children.

Her head and body would swing from side to side. For just a brief moment, La Llorona stopped and tried to snatch Doña Sofia's baby sister, but for some unknown reasons, she quickly changed her mind. La Llorona's face began to turn green and was glowing with a horrible, unearthly, transparent light. This was enough to send women and children and many men running inside their houses to lock their doors. The best weapon at their disposal was the power of praying.

    A few brave men and the local priest followed the weeping woman until she arrived at Lillian's Orchard. La Llorona made a large circle and started a huge bonfire without wood or matches. The fierce fire made loud, crackling sounds and threw sparks high and low. La Llorona floated into the center of the flames and was soon on fire. She was shrieking, moaning, and groaning. Finally, she let out piercing cries that carried into the night. The priest, not knowing what else to do, knelt and began praying. He clasped his rosary, pointing it toward La Llorona, and made the sign of the Holy Cross. "Let this Holy Cross help lead this weeping woman into finding eternal peace," he said as he closed his eyes. La Llorona, once again, let out a dreadful scream and her echoes made the people tremble. Jets of fire spurted out of her body, along with her blood. La Llorona's face was changing colors and she fell to the ground. La Llorona held her throat and made horrid, choking sounds as she began to shrink in size. Her satin dress became a bundle of rags and she withered until she lay lifeless on the ground. She took the shape of the trunk of an old wrinkled apple tree. Hours later, the priest and the men went home drained, weary, and tired. Maybe someday they would relate the story, but for now they just wanted to sleep and forget.

Doña Sofia ended her story with sadness as she wiped the tears from her eyes. Perhaps in death, La Llorona might have ended her eternal search for her children and be united with them forever.

Storytelling was not only a means for Mexican parents to prevent intolerable behavior among the children of the barrio, it was also a means to make us conscious of the world around us. Family values, principles, and objectives in life were instrumental in the shaping of our minds at a tender age through storytelling. The romantic story of Ramón, a poor man who had squandered all his riches and was now faced with impoverishment, and the well-to-do Flor, whose family deplored her relationship with him because he is poor, is another in a long line of typical *Cuentos from Long Ago*. As Paulette Atencio relates it, this story unveils some heartwarming thoughts of love at all costs, the dream of marriage, and the magical help from an unknown source!

The Magic Stones

A long time ago in a town called La Otra Banda, or "Other Side of the Valley," there lived a young and handsome man by the name of Ramón Ramírez. He had a reputation for being a fine horseman. His family was very wealthy. When his parents passed away, Ramón was the sole heir of the estate. Ramón was very kind to all the poor from the area. He was generous to a fault, and in a few years he too was a poor man.

In the surrounding area, there was a young lady named Flor Trujillo. Flor and Ramón were very much in love and wanted to get married. Flor came from a family that was not only very wealthy, but extremely political and influential. They owned most of the land and cattle in the area. Her parents would not allow Flor to marry Ramón because he was considered a poor and foolish man who had squandered all his riches. Flor's parents could not see their daughter living in a poor man's world. According to Flor's parents, the only way Ramón could marry their daughter was by becoming a wealthy man again. Ramón knew that this was impossible. It would take a miracle! All Ramón owned was an old house that was ready to fall and his white stallion horse called Bulto.

Flor's parents decided not to waste any more time on Ramón. An older but wealthy man from Santa Rosa had asked for Flor's hand in marriage, and Flor's parents had granted their permission. The wedding date was only two days away. Ramón decided to pay Flor's parents a visit to attempt to convince them that he was the man for their daughter.

It was dark and Ramón was riding toward La Otra Banda. He suddenly heard a loud voice shout, "Halt! Get off your horse and pick up some stones. Put them in your pocket. Soon you will be sad but glad." Ramón felt so stupid. He kept looking around wondering who could be talking to him. He finally sifted through the ground until he found a couple of small stones and he put them in his pocket. He got back on his horse and rode on.

After having ridden for about four miles, Ramón heard the same voice with the same command. Once again he obeyed, not knowing why. "Halt! Get off your horse! Pick up some stones! Put them in your pocket. Soon you will be sad but glad!" Again, Ramón felt stupid and kept looking around still trying to figure out who was talking to him. Again, Ramón sifted through the ground and found many stones and put them in his pockets. He remounted his horse and rode on.

Many miles later, Ramón heard the same voice with the same message. This time he picked up stones until his pockets were bulging, as were the inside of his jacket and shirt. By this time he thought it was funny and kept laughing to himself for being so stupid.

As Ramón approached Flor's home, the path became steep and dangerous. The stones in his pockets began to pinch and rub his legs. This was causing him great pain and his skin felt raw. Ramón began to take many of the stones from his pocket and threw them away. When Ramón arrived at Flor's house, he had forgotten all about the stones.

Flor was outside the house. She came running to greet him, threw her arms around him, and began to kiss him. Together, they went inside the house and told her parents of their decision to marry even without their approval. Flor's father became very angry and started shouting, demanding to know how Ramón was going to support their daughter in his state of poverty.

Ramón also lost his temper and shouted back, "I will support your daughter with all the stones I own!" Ramón was just trying to be funny and sarcastic. Without thinking, he emptied his pockets and placed all the stones on top of the table. All of a sudden, a miracle took place! The stones began to change. They were transformed into beautiful diamonds, gold nuggets, rubies, emeralds, and pearls. They all gasped in unison.

Everyone was wide eyed and could not believe what they had just witnessed!

At that moment Ramón was both sad and glad. He was sad that he had thrown away so many of the stones, but he was glad that he at least had kept enough to make his future in-laws change their minds! Flor's parents were now very happy and gave them their blessing. Ramón took Flor in his arms and kissed her. Since the wedding preparations were already in progress, Ramón and Flor were married almost immediately. They became very rich and lived happily ever after!

The Two Compadres

These were two compadres. One was rich and the other poor. The rich was very genial, and never a day passed that he didn't make it a point to greet his compadre and comadre. But further than an exchange of "Buenos días," he gave nothing; and since his compadre was very poor, his stinginess was resented.

"Vieja," said the poor man to his señora, "I've thought of a scheme. We must get money from our compadre. Go to the place where you grind masa and ask the family to lend us twenty cents; then buy a pen, ink, and paper. I shall go into the chaparral and catch two jackrabbits."

Within two hours rabbits, paper, ink, and pen were at hand. "Now, old woman," the poor compadre said, "sit just outside the door, and call to me when you see our compadre." Presently the señora said, "Here he comes."

The poor compadre seated himself quickly at the table and with pen in hand pretended to be very busy writing a letter.

"Buenos dias, comadre," the rich man greeted the woman. "¿Como le amanecio [How did you get up this morning]?"

"Very well, thanks, compadre. Only we have little to eat."

"And my compadre, where is he?" asked the rich man, ignoring the hint.

"Ai 'ta dentro," responded the comadre. "He is inside writing a setter to a friend in the city."

"Buenos dias, compadre," the poor man greeted the rich man. "You will pardon the delay in speaking to you. I am in a hurry to get a letter off to a friend in the city."

"Then I will not detain you, since you will need to hurry to the post office.

"No, señor compadre," responded the poor man. "I don't mail any letters. I have a rabbit that is trained to run errands. He does the job quicker and saves me stamps." Thereupon the poor compadre tied the letter to the rabbit's neck and turned him loose. The Rich compadre was surprised at the speed with which the pet tool off down the flat. "When will he return from the city?" he asked.

"Not later than tomorrow," said the poor compadre. "You see how he runs. Neither hound nor hawk will stop him."

"Marvelous," said the rich man. "I shall return tomorrow to learn more about this wonderful rabbit. If he's as good as you say, I must buy him."

The following day the poor compadre said to his señora, "Look, vieja, sit just outside the door and call to me when you see our compadre." She sat and presently said, "There comes our compadre."

Then the poor compadre brought in the other rabbit and ran him about the room until he was almost winded and was panting like a horse with the thumps.

"Buenos días, comadre," said the rich man as he entered. "Has my compadre's pet returned yet with the mail?"

"Sí, señor. Come in; it has just this instant arrived. Your compadre is reading the letter now."

"Quiubo, compadre," called the poor man. "Pase, hombre. Only look at this! Good time, don't you think?" He handed the rich man a letter addressed to himself that he had just that morning faked.

"And look how winded my rabbit is! Once on the flat he travels like the wind."

"Pues, sí," said the rich man, "it is all very good. However, you don't need him as I do. Sell him to me, compadre. How much will you take-one hundred dollars?"

"You know compadre, compadre, I would sooner sell him to you than anyone else; yet it is impossible. First, he's a pet; and second, I need him."

"But I need him worse," said the rich man. "I will give you five hundred dollars for him."

"No, compadre, I am sorry, but…"

The rich man compadre stooped quickly, picked up the rabbit, and said, "Adios, compadre. I'm taking him with me. If you want a thousand dollars, come to my house."

The deal was made, and the rich compadre began writing letters. His senora, too, wrote many letters. After a bit she said, "Mira, hijo, I must return these jewels to our friend in the city. Will our rabbit take them?"

"Como no?" said the man. "He's perfectly safe. He travels like the wind across the flat. Neither hound nor hawk will be able to stop him."

They made a package of the jewels and the letters and tied it to the rabbit's neck. He took off with a speed that amazed them both, and the man said, "You will see; tomorrow morning early he will back with the answers."

However, the morrow came and went and so did the day following without the rabbit's returning. The third day a cruel suspicion dawned upon the rich compadre, and he swore to get revenge.

In the meantime the poor compadre had been busy cooking another pie for his friend. "Vieja," he said to his wife, "take this peso to the market square and buy a beef's bladder and a quart of blood, and on the way home find some kind of rare flower. Bring these to me, and sit just outside the door and call to me when you see our compadre."

The flower, blood, and bladder were brought; and the man explained that the rich compadre would be very angry when he arrived and would likely want to fight.

"You," he said, "you put the bladder filled with blood beneath your blouse on the left side, and when we become noisy, come to me and say: 'Look, Viejo, you mustn't quarrel with my compadre. You two will end by becoming angry.' Then I will jump to my feet and stab the bladder and say, 'Woman of the devil attends to your own business.' Then you fall as if dead and our compadre will feel compromised. I will then take the flower and pass it before your face. You must sit up. I will do this again and you will stand. And on the third pass of the flower you will smile and say, 'I feel well again.'"

All being arranged to the finest detail, the comadre sat just outside the door. Presently she said, "A-a-a viene mi compadre."

The man pretended to be busy. "Buenos diás, comadre," said the rich man. "Is my compadre here? I must speak with him."

"Pase, compadre," said the poor man. The quarrel began immediately. One accused the other of fraud and the other denied the accusation.

"Look. Viejo," said the woman, "You mustn't quarrel with my compadre. You two will end by being angry." Thereupon the poor man sprang to his feet and stabbed her.

She fell to the floor, and the blood ran from the wound. "Dios mío!" said the rich man. "What have you done, compadre? They will hang us for this."

"Don't worry," said the poor man. "I have a magic flower of life, Behold."

He took the flower from his pocket and with the first pass before the wounded woman's face she sat up, with the second she stood, and with the third she said she was well again.

"Sell me that flower," said the rich compadre.

"No, compadre, I can't; I expect to go to the city, and once there I shall get rich curing people of all kinds of ills."

"I will give you one thousand dollars for your magic flower."

"No, compadre, something will go wrong, and then you will blame me."

"Blame you for what, compadre?" said the rich man. He snatched the flower from the poor man and said, "If you want twenty-five thousand dollars, come to my house."

The bargain was made.

"I saw our compadre leaving here," said the rich man's wife upon returning from mass. "You must have nothing to do with him. Remember the rabbit."

"Remember nothing," said the rich man. "Listen, woman of the devil, attend to your own business." Thereupon he stabbed her, and she fell to the floor. The daughter and the servants began to weep. "Shut up, you" said the man.

"It is nothing. I have a magic flower of life. Behold, and you will see her come alive."

He passed the flower before the dead one's face. But she did not sit up. He repeated this and she did not stand. He repeated it once more and she did not speak. She was dead, de versax.

"Ay, ay, ay," wailed the man. "So soon as I shall have buried my senora, I shall go immediately and kill my compadre." In the meantime the poor man was setting another trap for his compadre.

"Vieja," he said, "get four candles and a large white cloth. Your compadre will be here soon, and I must play dead." Candles and cloth were brought. The man laid himself flat on the floor and crossed his hands over his chest. The woman covered him with the sheet and put two lighted candles at the head and two at the feet. Then she sat just outside the door and presently said,

"Ay-a-a viene mi compadre," And the man lay as still as death. "Buenos dias, comadre," said the rich man. The woman began weeping bitterly and did not return the greeting. "What is the matter, comadre?" said the rich man.

"Your-your- compadre is dead," said she. The rich man removed his hat and entered the room. "Too bad, comadre. What killed my compadre?"

"Too-too-toothache," wept the woman.

"Ha!" said the rich man. "Strange that he should die of toothache. Living or dead, however, I think I shall take him with me." Thereupon he unfolded a large sack, and slipped it over the body of his compadre and tied it securely. Just then he heard a burro passing by, and he called to the two arrieros driving it to help with the sack and its contents. They placed the load on the animal and made off calle arriba (up the street) for the rich man's home.

Upon arriving there he told the arrieros to wait until he saddled his horse. He entered his corral and left them at the gate.

"I wonder what is in this sack," whispered an arriero.

"Ay-ay," came a voice from within "take me down and I'll tell." They removed the sack from the burro.

"Ay, ay," came the voice, "untie the sack and I'll tell." They untied the sack.

"Ay, ay," said the man, "lift me to my feet and I'll tell."

They lifted him and he said, "My compadre is trying to compel me to marry a rich girl. Though I explained that I have a family he wouldn't listen, and for that you see me here."

"I'm not married," said an arriero. "I will marry the rich girl for you, con mucho gusto."

They placed the arriero in the sack; and before the poor man escaped calle abaja (down the street), he had them promise to say nothing to the rich compadre about the change. Presently the rich man returned, all booted and spurred and ready to ride.

"Where is your friend?" he asked the arriero. "He had some business to attend to and asked me stay and helps you."

"Here are ten pesos," said the rich man. "I won't need you now. Leave the burro to me."

He drove to the sea, removed the load, and dumped it into the water. Then he returned to town and sat in front of his house to read a newspaper. Presently he saw seated against the wall just across the street another man.

"For the life of me," he said, "it is my compadre. Oiga, you, listen, compadre; come over here. How did you make out, compadre?"

"I'm provoked," said the poor man. "You dumped me into the sea but not far enough out. Look!"

When released from the sack at the corral gate, the poor compadre had gone home and thence to the thickets. While he was there, fate so had it that he found the jewels the rabbit had lost. "Look at these pearls," said he. "The ocean bed is covered with them, and the people of the sea gave me these before I came away."

"What?" said the rich? "I must have some jewels like that. compadre, do me the favor to tie me in a sack and dump me into the ocean at the very place where you fell."

"No compadre," said the poor man. "Something will go wrong and you will blame me."

"By no means, friend. Look, I will put my hacienda in trust for you. Do me this one great favor, compadre."

"Very well," said the poor man. The trust was made; the rich compadre was duly sacked and dumped into the sea in accordance with his own wishes, and the poor compadre is now rich. He is held in great esteem by the people of his town for many innocent little pranks.

The Little Match Girl

It was so terribly cold. Snow was falling, and it was almost dark. Evening came on, the last evening of the year. In the cold and gloom a poor little girl, bareheaded and barefoot, was walking through the streets. Of course when she had left her house she'd had slippers on, but what good had they been? They were very big slippers, way too big for her, for they belonged to her mother. The little girl had lost them running across the road, where two carriages had rattled by terribly fast. One slipper she'd not been able to find again, and a boy had run off with the other, saying he could use it very well as a cradle some day when he had children of his own. And so the little girl walked on her naked feet, which were quite red and blue with the cold. In an old apron she carried several packages of matches, and she held a box of them in her hand. No one had bought any from her all day long, and no one had given her a cent.

Shivering with cold and hunger, she crept along, a picture of misery, poor little girl! The snowflakes fell on her long fair hair, which hung in pretty curls over her neck. In all the windows lights were shining, and there was a wonderful smell of roast goose, for it was New Year's Eve. Yes, she thought of that!

In a corner formed by two houses, one of which projected farther out into the street than the other, she sat down and drew up her little feet under her. She was getting colder and colder, but did not dare to go home, for she had sold no matches, nor earned a single cent, and her father would surely beat her. Besides, it was cold at home, for they had nothing over them but a roof through which the wind whistled even though the biggest cracks had been stuffed with straw and rags.

Her hands were almost dead with cold. Oh, how much one little match might warm her! If she could only take one from the box and rub it against the wall and warm her hands. She drew one out. R-r-ratch! How it sputtered and burned! It made a warm, bright flame, like a little candle, as she held her hands over it; but it gave a strange light! It really seemed to the little girl as if she were sitting before a great iron stove with shining brass knobs and a brass cover. How wonderfully the fire burned! How comfortable it was! The youngster stretched out her feet to warm them too; then the little flame went out, the stove vanished, and she had only the remains of the burnt match in her hand.

She struck another match against the wall. It burned brightly, and when the light fell upon the wall it became transparent like a thin veil, and she could see through it into a room. On the table a snow-white cloth was spread, and on it stood a shining dinner service. The roast goose steamed gloriously, stuffed with apples and prunes. And what was still better, the goose jumped down from the dish and waddled along the floor with a knife and fork in its breast, right over to the little girl. Then the match went out, and she could see only the thick, cold wall. She lighted another match. Then she was sitting under the most beautiful Christmas tree. It was much larger and much more beautiful than the one she had seen last Christmas through the glass door at the rich merchant's home. Thousands of candles burned on the green branches, and colored pictures like those in the print shops looked down at her. The little girl reached both her hands toward them. Then the match went out. But the Christmas lights mounted higher. She saw them now as bright stars in the sky. One of them fell down, forming a long line of fire.

"Now someone is dying," thought the little girl, for her old grandmother, the only person who had loved her, and who was now dead, had told her that when a star fell down a soul went up to God.

She rubbed another match against the wall. It became bright again, and in the glow the old grandmother stood clear and shining, kind and lovely.

"Grandmother!" cried the child. "Oh, take me with you! I know you will disappear when the match is burned out. You will vanish like the warm stove, the wonderful roast goose and the beautiful big Christmas tree!"

And she quickly struck the whole bundle of matches, for she wished to keep her grandmother with her. And the matches burned with such a glow that it became brighter than daylight. Grandmother had never been so grand and beautiful. She took the little girl in her arms, and both of them flew in brightness and joy above the earth, very, very high, and up there was neither cold, nor hunger, nor fear-they were with God.

But in the corner, leaning against the wall, sat the little girl with red cheeks and smiling mouth, frozen to death on the last evening of the old year. The New Year's sun rose upon a little pathetic figure. The child sat there, stiff and cold, holding the matches, of which one bundle was almost burned.

"She wanted to warm herself," the people said. No one imagined what beautiful things she had seen, and how happily she had gone with her old grandmother into the bright New Year.

Sayings from Our Grandparents

Proverbs and sayings are an important part of life. They contribute immeasurably to a child's education. They stay in our minds and we remember them throughout our lives. Here are some we heard in the barrio. Please bear in mind that some things are lost in translation.

"Lo hecho, no puede ser deshecho." (That which is already done cannot be changed.)

"Labrador que estima su fama, que no salga el sol estando en su cama." (Laborer, who esteems his fame, let not the sun come out if he is in bed.)

"Para aprender, es necesario a veces perder." (To learn, it is necessary to sometimes lose.)

"A quien es cerrado de intelecto, de poco le sirven los libros abiertos." (He who is devoid of intellect, to him, the opened books are of little use.)

"El toro y el melón, así como salen son." (The bull and the melón arrive as they are.)

"En la tierra como en el mar, se ahoga el que no sabe nadar." (In land or sea, you'll drown if you can't swim.)

"Gato escaldado del agua fría huye." (The cautious or suspicious cat flees cold water.)

"Ni están todos los que son, ni son…todos los que están." (Nor are they here whom they are, nor…are they here whom should be.)

"Dime lo que aborreces, y te diré de que careces." (Tell me what you despise, and I'll tell what you lack.)

"Quien mucho abarca poco aprieta." (He who embarks on too much, grabs very little.)

"Agua que no has de beber, déjala correr." (Water thou canst drink, let it run its path.)

"Cantar en tinaja." (To be fond of one's own praise.)

"De refranes y cantares, tiene el pueblo mil millares.) (Of proverbs and songs, the village has a thousandfold.)

"Cantar a libro abierto." (To sing offhand.)

"Cantar de plano." (To make a plain and full confession.)

"Cantar la Victoria." (To triumph.)

"Cantarle a uno la potra." (To predict a change of weather by bodily pains.)

"Cantar misa." (To say the first mass.)

"Ese es otro cantar." (That is another kind of speech.)

"Cantar mal y porfiar." (To chatter nonsense.)

"¡Lo digo cantado o rezado!" (How would you have me say it?)

"Al fin se canta la Gloria." (Do not triumph till all is over or Don't whistle before you are out of the woods.)

Chiquillados

"Chiquillados" are short verses recited by a man either to amuse or to impress a woman he wanted to dance with. If the woman accepted the verse, she would get up and dance. The chiquillados, which rhyme like some dichos and proverbs, sound better in Spanish, and although they no longer rhyme in English, they retain their meaning. However, in the process of translation, they may lose their charm.

Anoche fuí a tu casa
tres golpes le di al candado
tú no sirves para amores,
tienes el sueño pesado.

Anoche fuí a tu casa,
me salieron todos los perros,

fuí a levantar una piedra,
y me embarré todos los dedos.
Anoche tuve un sueño que
me ha servido de risa,
soñe que estaba en tus brazos,
y recordé en la ceniza.

Last night, I went to your house,
I knocked three times,
You aren't good for love
Because you sleep too heavily

Last night I went to your house,
and the dogs went after me,

FÉLIX VALENZUELA

I went to pick up a rock,
and I got my fingers all dirty.
Last night, I had a dream
that has helped me to laugh.
I dreamt that I was in your arms,
and I woke up in the cinders.

Aunque tu padre me diera	Even if your father would give me
los bueyes y la carreta,	the oxen and the cart,
no me he de casar contigo,	I would never marry you,
ojos de borrega prieta.	eyes of a black sheep.
De esta flor	From this flower
y de esta rosa,	and this rose,
señora, usted es coja.	Madam, you are lame.

Mexican Riddles—"Adivinanzas"

"Adivinanzas" are riddles designed to test our ability to identify familiar sights, surroundings, objects, and even people. They were an important part of education in the barrio. Although the riddles seem to be simple on the surface, they contained language that was above the slang used in the barrio. We looked up to the people who recited adivinanzas. We thought they were knowledgeable and wise, worthy to be our instructors

Blanco salí de me (mi) casa,
y en el campo enverdeci,
Para volver a entrar en mi casa,
De rojo me vesti.
(Respuesta: chile)

Entre medio de dos paredes blancas
Estaba una cuenda amarilla
El que no me lo adivina ahora,
no me lo adivina en todo el día.
(Respusta: un huevo).

En una noria muy honda
Hay un cabresto muy largo,
Destendido no alcanza,
Doblado hasta sobra.
(Respuesta: la noria es la boca y el cabresto es el brazo)

I left my house in white,
I returned green in the countryside,
To return to my house,
I dressed in red.

FÉLIX VALENZUELA

(Answer: chile)

There was a yellow bead
between two white walls
Whoever doesn't guess it now won't guess it all day.
(Answer: an egg)

There was a very long rope
in a very deep well,
While stretched out it doesn't reach,
And folded up, there is some left over.
(Answer: the well is the mouth and the rope is the arm)

The Mexican and Cristero revolutions.

The Songs of the Mexican Revolution

My grandfather, Jesus Carreon, was 106 years old when he passed away in Compton, California, during the late 1980s. Recruited at a tender age to serve under Gen. Pancho Villa, he was in company with others around the campfires built by the Mexican troops where the most popular and traditional Mexican songs of today were composed. The soldiers sang them during their stops along the pathways of the revolution.

In his later years, my grandpa loved to listen to these Mexican songs because of the memories they brought him of Mexico's revolution. Most of the lyrics were light and gay, but some reflected real life in the regiments and sometimes alluded to the grim reality of war. Most of the songs were romantic, some included melancholy sadness, and all were sympathetic to the Mexican soldier's struggle for peace and harmony.

Death was always present in the lives of the revolutionary men, and the songs told stories about the unfortunate separation of the Mexican male from his woman. One particularly emotional song, "La Barca de Oro" ("The Golden Boat") tells of the man's death during the revolution and his impending trip on the golden boat:

> Yo ya me voy al puerto donde se halla,
> (I am now departing to the port where)
> la barca de oro, que debe conducirme,
> (the golden boat lies, which will guide me)
> Yo ya me voy, solo vengo a despedirme,
> (I leave now, I come alone to say good-bye)
> Adiós, mujer, adiós para siempre, adiós.
> (Good-bye, woman; good-bye forever; good-bye)
> No volverán, mis ojos a mirarte; ni tus
> (My eyes will see you no more;)

oídos, escucharán mi canto,
(nor will you hear my song ever again)
Voy a aumentar, los mares con mi llanto,
(I shall fill the oceans with my anguish)
Adiós, mujer, adiós, para siempre, adios.
(Good-bye, woman; good-bye forever; goodbye)

Similarly, the sentimental songs "La Valentina" and "Mariquita Linda Adiós" express the feelings of soldiers as they leave for battle and leave behind the dear and sacred things they cherish the most:

La Valentina

Valentina, Valentina, yo te quisiera decir; que una pasión me domina,
(Valentina, Valentina, I wish to tell you that a passion overpowers me)
y es la que me hizo venir.
(it is the reason for my being here)
Dicen que por tus amores, la vida me han de quitar, no le hace
(They say that because of your love, they can do away with my life, it doesn't matter)
que sean muy diablos, yo también me se pelear.
(let them do me wrong, I can defend myself.)
Valentina, Valentina, rendido estoy a tus pies; si es porque me ves
(Valentina, Valentina, I render myself at your feet if it's because you see me)
borracho, mañana ya no me ves.
(drunken, tomorrow you will see me no more)
Sí es porque tomo tequila, mañana tomo jerez; si me han de matar
(If it is because I drink tequila, tomorrow I'll drink sherry.)
Mañana, que me maten de una vez.
(Tomorrow, they can kill me once and for all.)

FÉLIX VALENZUELA

Mariquita Linda Adios

Adiós, Mariquita Linda, ya me voy porque tu ya no me quieres como yo te quiero a ti.

(Farewell, beautiful Mariquita, I leave because you love me no more as I love you.)

Adiós, chaparrita chula, ya me voy para tierras muy lejanas y ya nunca volveré.

(Farewell, my tiny, delightful one, to distant lands I go, and I shall never return.)

Adiós, mida de mi vida, la causa de mis dolores.

(Farewell, soul of my life, the cause of all my pain.)

El amor de mis amores, el perfume de mis flores, para siempre dejare.

(The love of my loves, the perfume of my flowers, forever I leave now.)

St. Valentine's Day Celebration

Here is an interesting commentary along with a charming history of Valentine's Day.

St. Valentine's Day in Hispanic culture was a very special day of celebration. Unlike the typical exchange of romantically versed Valentine's cards commonly purchased in the stores, this day, as in other festive occasions, brought the family together for hot "champurrado" (sweetened flour-based drink) or "bebida de horchata" (a resin or mixture of sweetened white rice and milk) and tequila (alcoholic beverage) for the adults, "caldo de rez" (a soup with meat, vegetables, potatoes, and corn similar to beef stew but without the gravy mixture) and sharing romantic tales about life in Mexico. It also caused bonding between families and gave us a memorable time for us to reacquaint with each other, both young and old. Also, it was a time for the younger members to enjoy storytelling and good food.

Today, chocolate sweets, flowers, and paper valentines inscribed with romantic thoughts and verses are mostly exchanged between kids at school, as well as in the workplace, but rarely at home. A common sight today portrays kids returning home from school bragging about all the valentines received. Typically, it is a time for boyfriends to spend money out of their pockets on chocolates for their sweethearts. Storytelling and the gathering of families for St. Valentine's Day is a thing of the past. This day has become a more personalized event each year. A gratifying kiss from husband to wife or between other sweethearts, especially among the youth, is now the anticipated trend or expected outcome. It has completely lost the spiritual significance that it originally had.

The history of St. Valentine's Day started in the third century with the entry of a tyrant Roman emperor and a humble Christian martyr. The emperor was Claudius II. The Christian was Valentine. The emperor had declared that the socializing of people with

Christians was considered a crime punishable by death. Valentine, who had dedicated his entire life to the practice of Christian ideals, was not afraid of the threats imposed by Claudius II. He was not afraid of the tyrant emperor and did not refrain from engaging in the practices of his belief.

Consequently, one day, Valentine was arrested and sent to prison. While there, one of the prison guards fraternized with him and thereafter started bringing his blind daughter, whose name was Julia, to listen to Valentine's narration of historical Roman stories. As time passed, Valentine taught Julia in a variety of subject matters and introduced her to mathematics and things pertaining to God. Julia began to know the world very well through the guiding eyes of Valentine. One pleasant day, Julia asked him, "Valentine, is it true that God listens to our prayers?"

To which he responded, "Yes, my tiny friend. He listens to all of them and also to all of our supplications."

"Do you know what I ask God for every night and every morning? I pray to be able to see. I want to see with my own eyes all that you have told me."

Valentine, who listened attentively to Julia's words, told her, "God always does what's best for all of us if we believe in him."

Both knelt together while holding hands and began to pray. Suddenly, an indescribable light illuminated the prison cell, causing Julia to exclaim, "Valentine, I can see. I can see!"

The passage of time found Valentine at the point of death, writing a letter to Julia, whom he signed with the following ending, "from your Valentine." Finally, Valentine was executed the next day on February 14, in the year 270, near a door, which was later known as Valentine's Door in his honor.

Valentine was buried in what is now known as the Church of Praxedes in Rome. According to legend, Julia planted an almond of red roses in the same area symbolizing love and eternal friendship. Every fourteenth of February, St. Valentine's Day inspires messages of love, affection, and devotion around the world.

Honoring the Dead

The Day of the Dead celebrations in Mexico can be traced back to a pre-Columbian past. Rituals celebrating the deaths of ancestors had been observed by these civilizations, perhaps for as long as 2,500–3,000 years. In the pre-Hispanic era, skulls were commonly kept as trophies and displayed during the rituals to symbolize death and rebirth.

The festival that became the modern Day of the Dead fell in the ninth month of the Aztec calendar, about the beginning of August, and was celebrated for an entire month. The festivities were dedicated to the goddess known as the Lady of the Dead, corresponding to the modern Catrina.

In most regions of Mexico, November 1 is to honor children and infants; whereas, deceased adults are honored on November 2. This is indicated by generally referring to November 1 mainly as Día de los Inocentes (Day of the Innocents) but also as Día de los Angelitos (Day of the Little Angels), and November 2 as Día de los Muertos or Día de los Difuntos (Day of the Dead).

People go to cemeteries to be with the souls of the departed and build private altars containing the favorite foods and beverages as well as photos and memorabilia of the departed. The intent is to encourage visits by the souls, so the souls will hear the prayers and the comments of the living directed to them. Celebrations can take a humorous tone as celebrants remember funny events and anecdotes about the departed.

Plans for the day are made throughout the year, including gathering the goods to be offered to the dead. During the three-day period, families usually clean and decorate graves; most visit the cemeteries where their loved ones are buried and decorate their graves with "ofrendas" (altars), which often include orange Mexican marigolds (*Tagetes erecta*) called "cempasúchil" (originally named *cempoaxochitl*, Nahuatl for "twenty flowers").

In modern Mexico, this name is sometimes replaced with the term "flor de muerto" (flower of dead). These flowers are thought to attract souls of the dead to the offerings.

Toys are brought for dead children ("los angelitos" or the little angels) and bottles of tequila, mezcal or pulque or jars of atole for adults. Families will also offer trinkets or the deceased's favorite candies on the grave. Ofrendas are also put in homes, usually with foods such as candied pumpkin, "pan de muerto" (bread of dead), and sugar skulls, and beverages such as atole. The ofrendas are left out in the homes as a welcoming gesture for the deceased. Some people believe the spirits of the dead eat the spiritual essence of the ofrendas food, so though the celebrators eat the food after the festivities, they believe it lacks nutritional value. Pillows and blankets are left out so the deceased can rest after their long journey. In some parts of Mexico, such as the towns of Mixquic, Pátzcuaro and Janitzio, people spend all night beside the graves of their relatives. In many places, people have picnics at the gravesite as well.

Las Posadas—Reenacting Joseph and Mary's Journey

The Posadas experience is a special celebration of the birth of Jesus. It is primarily celebrated in Latin American countries and in the United States by Catholics who speak the Spanish language. In El Paso, the public is always invited to take part in the Posadas taking place in the Lower Valley on the Mission Trail. Basically, a group of people gather to enact the trip Joseph and Mary made to find lodgings in Bethlehem. They carry candles, maybe statues of Joseph and Mary, perhaps someone rides on a donkey. The idea is to reenact the famous journey. The group then goes from house to house asking for lodging. They sing songs, and the people inside the house also sing songs, telling the procession there is no room for them in the house. Finally, at the last house, the homeowners invite them inside. They all sing songs of celebration and received various sweets and drinks especially made for the occasion.

Two Mexicans Visit Jerusalem

A dmonishments and exhortations were continually made by the older generation as means of prevention against the barrio's Mexican inhabitants falling into oblivion. Their admonitions were expressive, colorful, realistic, and meant to convey warnings, sometimes in the most bizarre and obscure manner. They invoked upon us the resolve to utilize our mental capabilities first before embarking on a journey in life. Hence, we were instructed to "usar la chompa" (slang for use your best intellectual understanding and/or your brain) as often as possible before undertaking roles in pursuit of probable perilous activities:

It is said that in the thirty-third year of our Lord, two Mexicans visited Jerusalem. On the day that they arrived, there was a great commotion in the streets. Hoards of people were moving in one direction. One of the Mexican visitors, guided as always by the wisdom of his people, asked his compa (companion), "Where are you going, Vicente (Vincent)? And where are all the people going!" They joined the crowds and arrived before a disturbing spectacle. There, on a hill, one man was hanging on a cross.

Vicente said, "Look at what they are doing to the Lord!" He rushed toward the Lord and pulled out the nail that held one of his hands. He immediately went to the other side and pulled out the other nail. The Lord, held by the nails in his feet, clawed the air in desperation and fell face forward with a crash.

The moral of the story is that love is fine, but it must be efficacious love. On the other hand, there is the statement by a wise old Mexican, who said during the government of one of the presidents in Mexico, "Dios nos libre de los pendejos con iniciativa." The Spanish expression has more impact than its English equivalent, but might be translated as "There is nothing so dangerous as a fool in power" (source unknown).

Cinco de Mayo Celebration

On the fifth of May in the year 1862, loyal and truly patriotic Mexicans of the liberal persuasion, the Juaristas, in backing their Indian president, Benito Juarez, fought the first battle in their war against the French invaders and their disloyal Mexicans compatriots, the Conservatives. The Mexicans, that loyalty to their president and to the Mexican Constitution of 1857, met in open battle in the hills on the outskirts of the city of Puebla de los Angeles, ninety miles southeast of Mexico City. Six thousand strong, the French forces were advancing from Veracruz but were repelled by the Mexicans in a fierce battle and were forced to retreat to Veracruz.

Europe's finest army at the time, the French army, met defeat in Puebla. The poor Mexicans, no match for the grand army of the French emperor, Napoleon III, met the French head on in unrelenting frontal attacks. The ill-equipped Mexicans proved their mettle.

The Mexican regulars fought with arms they had used forty years earlier, in their War of Independence, as well as in their ill-fated war against the United States. They fought well and hard. As Mexicans are prone to say, "Las armas de Mexico se cubrieron de Gloria" (Mexican arms covered themselves with glory). The regulars, the campesinos (peasants), rancheros, Indios fought with whatever they could muster: machetes, lances, knives, slings, lassoes, and sticks, etcetera. The Mexicans indeed "covered themselves with glory." Their two young generals, Ignacio Zaragoza, a Mexican Texan born at Goliad, Texas, and the also brave young general for Oaxaca, Porfirio Diaz, led them to victory.

The whole world heard about the batalla del 5 de Mayo and how the Mexicans had defeated Napoleon's forces. One year later though, the French forces, thirty-thousand strong, plus their Conservative Mexican allies, attacked Puebla for the second time and took it. Then they proceeded to Mexico City, the capital, and occupied it.

Benito Juarez began his long pilgrimage to save his government, always just one step ahead of the French. From Mexico City, the French eventually spread out and occupied most of Mexico's major cities, but the countryside belonged to the Mexican guerrillas. It was a protracted guerrilla war. Benito Juarez and the loyal and true Mexicans kept on fighting until the would-be emperor, Fernando Maximiliano, Archduke of Austria, and his Mexican allies, the disloyal Conservatives, were defeated in the final big battle of the war, a two-month siege of Queretaro. The battle of Queretaro came to an end on May 15, 1867. Mexico was saved for the Mexicans. Thus, the reason for the celebration of Cinco de Mayo, a glorious and sacred day to Mexicans and their descendants.

The Sixteenth of September Celebration

On September 16, 1810, a Catholic priest named Miguel Hidalgo y Costilla and some Mexican-born Spaniards or criollos/mestizos and Amerindians in the town of Dolores, Guanajuato, initiated a revolt against Spanish occupation by ringing the bells of the local church to bring together people for one of the most crucial moments in Mexican history. That gathering was the stepping stone for Mexicans to rise and defend themselves against the Spanish colonial authorities. The Spanish "gachupines," Miguel Hidalgo claimed, had exploited Mexico's wealth for over three hundred years. Soon after, he rallied over fifty thousand followers to use stones, slings, and whatever crude armaments that were available to them to use in their fight against the Spaniards. That action by Hidalgo attracted revolutionaries as well. But not all followers had the same noble motives. Later, Guanajuato and Celaya lay in ruin under the slaughter of a mass of Spanish soldiers wrought by mestizos.

Eleven years of war and decades of revolutionary acts had led to a long unrest and violent social struggle. Inspired by Hidalgo's famous cry for independence, "El grito de Dolores" became synonymous with "Mexicanos, viva Mexico!" The eventual defeat of Spain brought forth the long-awaited return of peace and is an affirmation of their patriotism. It can be said that the struggle for Mexican independence dates back to the decades after the Spanish conquest of the Aztec empire, when Martin Cortés, son of Hernán Cortés and La Malinche, led a revolt against the Spanish colonial government in order to eliminate the issues of oppression and privileges of the conquistadores.

After the abortive Conspiracy of the Machetes in 1799, the War of Independence was far from gaining unanimous support among

Mexicans that became divided between independents, autonomists, and royalists and/or an unlikely alliance between liberals and conservatives. Miguel Hidalgo y Costilla was captured, tried, and executed by the gachupines. Hidalgo was honored with the grand title of the father of Mexican independence.

Following the death of Father Hidalgo, the leadership of the evolutionary army was assumed by José Maria Morelos. Under his leadership, the cities of Oaxaca and Acapulco were occupied. In 1813, the Congress of Chilpancingo was convened and on November 6 of that year. The Congress signed the first official document of independence, known as the Solemn Act of the Declaration of Independence of Northern America. It was followed by a long period of war at the Siege of Cuautla. In 1815, Morelos was captured by Spanish colonial authorities, tried, and executed for treason in San Cristóbal Ecatepec on December 22.

Halloween

This is only part of an extensive, well-documented article about the origin and customs of Halloween. I believe this subject really requires an in-depth study.

> Today's Halloween customs are…thought to have been influenced by Christian dogma and practices derived from it. Halloween falls on the evening before the Christian holy days of All Hallows' Day (also known as All Saints', Hallowmas or Hallowtide) on 1 November and All Souls' Day on 2 November, thus giving the holiday on 31 October the full name of All Hallows' Eve (meaning the evening before All Hallows' Day). Since the time of the primitive Church, major feasts in the Christian Church (such as Christmas, Easter and Pentecost) had vigils which began the night before, as did the feast of All Hallows'. These three days are collectively referred to as Hallowtide and are a time for honoring the saints and praying for the recently departed souls who have yet to reach Heaven. All Saints was introduced in the year 609, but was originally celebrated on 13 May. In 835, it was switched to 1 November (the same date as Samhain) at the behest of Pope Gregory IV. Some suggest this was due to Celtic influence, while others suggest it was a Germanic idea. It is also suggested that the change was made on the "practical grounds that Rome in summer could not accommodate the great number of pilgrims who flocked to it."

By the end of the 12th century they had become holy days of obligation across Europe and involved such traditions as ringing church bells for the souls in purgatory. In addition, "it was customary for criers dressed in black to parade the streets, ringing a bell of mournful sound and calling on all good Christians to remember the poor souls." "Souling," the custom of baking and sharing soul cakes for all christened souls, has been suggested as the origin of trick-or-treating. The custom dates back at least as far as the 15th century and was found in parts of England, Belgium, Germany, Austria and Italy. Groups of poor people, often children, would go door-to-door during Hallow tide, collecting soul cakes as a means of praying for souls in purgatory. Shakespeare mentions the practice in his comedy The Two Gentlemen of Verona (1593). The custom of wearing costumes has been explicated by Prince Sorie Conteh, who wrote: "It was traditionally believed that the souls of the departed wandered the earth until All Saints' Day, and All Hallows' Eve provided one last chance for the dead to gain vengeance on their enemies before moving to the next world. In order to avoid being recognized by any soul that might be seeking such vengeance, people would don masks or costumes to disguise their identities." In the middle Ages, churches displayed the relics of martyred saints and those parishes that were too poor to have relics let parishioners dress up as the saints instead, a practice that some Christians continue in Halloween celebrations today. Academic folklorist Kingsley Palmer, in addition to others, has suggested that the carved jack-o'-lantern, a popular symbol of Halloween, originally represented the souls of the dead. On Halloween, in medieval Europe, "fires [were] lit to guide these souls on their way and deflect them from haunting honest Christian folk." In addition, households in Austria, England, and Ireland often had "candles burning in every room to guide the souls back to visit their earthly homes". These were known as "soul lights." Many Christians in continental Europe, especially in France, acknowledged "a belief that once a year, on Hallowe'en, the dead of the churchyards rose for one wild, hideous carnival," known as the danse macabre, which has been commonly depicted in church decoration, especially on the walls of cathedrals, monasteries, and cemeteries. Christopher Allmand and Rosamond McKitterick write in The New Cambridge Medieval History that "Christians were moved by the sight of the Infant Jesus playing on his mother's knee; their hearts were touched by the Pietà; and patron saints reassured them by their presence. But, all the while, the danse macabre urged them not to forget the end of all earthly things." This danse macabre, which was enacted by "Christian village children [who] celebrated the vigil of All Saints" in the 16th Century, has been suggested as the predecessor of modern day costume parties on this same day.

Matachines

M atachines (Spanish "matachín," a sword dancer in a fantastic costume — called also bouffon bpl matachi·ni [MexSp matachín, fr. Sp, matachin (sense 1a), fr. It mattaccino]: a member of a society of north and South American-Indian dancers who perform ritual dances). They are found from Peru up to Northern New Mexico where the Spanish first influenced the New World and introduced Christianity to the native peoples.

The Matachina dance or Danza de Matachines (Spanish) is explained through oral tradition among most Indian tribes as "The Dance of the Moors and Christians" and is the first masked dance introduced by the Spaniards. The Moors were driven out of Spain in 1492, and the missionaries introduced the dance to show the superiority of the Christians. The dance was adopted by the people, and today, many forms of this dance still exist. Though the dance steps vary among tribes, the dance formations are all similar. Masks continue to be used, but the style changes from village to village or tribe.

The introduction of the Dance of the Moors and Christians gave rise to a further range of masked dances, one of them recounting the Spanish victory over the Indians and their eventual conversion to Christianity. These dances are called conquest dances (also a Matachin tradition), and Cortes and La Malinche (his Indian mistress and translator) often appear in them. It's interesting to note that in many versions of this dance, the Indians wear lavish costumes while the Christians are played by children.

The Matachines dance for a deeper religious purpose, since most of them join to venerate either Mother Mary (Our Lady of Guadalupe, Our Lady of Lourdes, Immaculate Conception, etc.), a saint (the group usually chooses the saint that pertains to the church they belong to), or simply to worship Christ or God the Holy Trinity demonstrated by the three fork symbolized as a Sword of the Holy a Trinity.

Dressed in traditional ceremonial dress and clothing, the chief characters are El Monarca the monarch (Montezuma); the captains (usually consist of two–four and are Montezuma's main generals); La Malinche or Malintzin, the Indian mistress of Hernán Cortés; El Toro, the bull, the malevolent comic man of the play (also symbolizes Satan, or the devil, according to Roman Catholic religious interpretations) dressed in the skins of the buffalo and wearing the horns of this sacred ancestor; Abuelo, the grandfather; and Abuela, grandmother. With the help of a chorus of dancers, they portray the desertion of his people by Montezuma, the luring of him back by the wiles and smiles of La Malinche, the final reunion of king and people and the killing of El Toro, who is supposed to have made all the mischief. Much symbolism is seen in these groups. The most basic symbol of the dance is good versus evil with good prevailing.

All of the cultural artifacts associated with the dance are blessed by a priest. The dances are performed by the Matachines have significant symbolism. (*Wikipedia*)

Quinceañeras

The "quinceañera" is the celebration of a girl's fifteenth birthday marking her transition from childhood to young womanhood. In Mexico and in the Spanish-speaking areas of the United States, we understand the ceremony to be similar to a sweet sixteen party or a debutante's coming-out party. The details vary from country to country, and some celebrations may be more religious than others. *Wikipedia* gives a picture of the ideal ceremony; however, the true-to-life situation usually depends on the money available.

In Mexico, the birthday girl, known as the quinceañera, is adorned with elegant makeup. Traditionally, this would be the first time she would wear makeup, but today, this is not usually the case. The quinceañera is also expected to wear a formal evening dress. Traditionally, that dress is a long ball gown.

The Bencomo family.

In the Mexican tradition, when the teenager is Catholic, the quinceañera celebration begins with a thanksgiving mass. She arrives at the celebration accompanied by her parents, godparents, and court of honor. The court of honor is a group of her chosen peers consisting of paired-off girls and boys, respectively known as "damas" (dames) and "chambelanes" (chamberlains). Typically, there are seven or fourteen pairs of damas and chambelanes. At this religious mass, a rosary or sometimes a necklace with a locket or pendant depicting Mexico's patron saint, the Virgin of Guadalupe, is awarded to the teenager by her godparents, the a necklace having been previously blessed by the church clergy. She is also awarded a tiara. The tiara serves as a reminder that to her loved ones, especially her immediate family, the quinceañera will always be a princess; however, some also see it as denoting that she is a princess before God and the world. After this, the girl may leave her bouquet of flowers on the altar for the Virgin Mary.

After the thanksgiving mass, guests gather for a reception where the remaining celebratory events meant to honor the quinceañera will take place, including the rendering of gifts. This reception may be held at the quinceañera's home at an events room (such as a dining hall, banquet hall, or casino), or in some cases, publicly held, similar to a block party. During the reception, the birthday girl usually dances a traditional waltz with her "chambelane de honor," who is her chosen escort, and her court of honor. Often this section of the celebration is previously practiced and/or choreographed, often weeks in advance, sometimes even in several months in anticipation of the event. The basic reception consists of six major parts with dances taking place while a traditional Mexican meal is served:

- The formal entry – a grand entrance made by the quinceañera once most guests have been seated.
- The formal toast – an optional but usually featured part of the reception, generally initiated by the parents or godparents of the birthday girl.
- The first dance – usually a waltz where the girl dances, starting with her father.

- The family dance – usually a waltz involving just the immediate relatives, the chambelanes, godparents, and the closest friends of the girl.
- The preferred song – any modern song particularly enjoyed by the quinceañera is played and danced.
- The general dance – also usually a waltz, where everyone dances to a musical waltz tune.

Traditionally, Mexican girls could not dance in public until they turned fifteen, except at school dances or at family events. Therefore, the quinceañera's waltz with the chambelanes is the girl's first public dance.

Some families may choose to add ceremonial components to the celebration, depending on local customs. Among them are the ceremony of the changing of shoes, in which a family member presents the quinceañera with her first pair of high heel shoes; the crowning ceremony, in which a close relative vests her with a crown on her head; and the "ceremonia de la ultima muñeca" (literally, ceremony of the last doll), during which her father presents her with a doll usually wearing a dress similar to the quinceañera herself. The ceremony of the last doll is based on a Maya tradition and is related to the birthday girl's receipt and renouncement of the doll as she grows into womanhood. Likewise, the ceremony of the changing of shoes symbolizes the girl's passage into maturity.

Once all symbolic gestures have taken place, the dinner commences. At this point, the celebration reaches its high point. Contracted musical groups begin playing music, keeping the guests entertained. The music is played while the guests dine, chat, mingle, and dance.

The next morning, the family and closest friends may also attend a special breakfast, especially if they are staying with the family. Sometimes what is known as a recalentado (rewarming) takes place using any food not consumed during the event of the night before it is warmed again for a brunch-type event.

Mexican Mariachis

Apparently, the origin of the term "mariachi" has been disputed since at least the nineteenth century when Maximiliano was the French emperor of Mexico. Myth has it that the term Mariachi was a result of the French word for marriage or wedding added to the word for a particular celebration. But this too is disputed by some linguists who believe the word Mariachi predated the time when the French arrived in Mexico.

Mariachi is a form of folk music from Mexico. Mariachi began as a regional folk style called "son jaliscience" in the central west of Mexico originally played only with string instruments and musicians dressed in the white pants and shirts of peasant farmers. From the nineteenth to twentieth century, migrations from rural areas into cities, such as Guadalajara and Mexico City along with the Mexican government's cultural promotion, gradually relabeled it as Son style with its alternative name of mariachi, becoming used for the urban form. Modifications of the music include influences from other music such as polkas and waltzes, the addition of trumpets, and the use of charro outfits by mariachi musicians. The musical style began to take on national prominence in the first half of the twentieth century with its promotion at presidential inaugurations and on the radio in the 1920s.

Mariachi can refer to the music, the group, or just one musician. Prior to the arrival of the Spanish, indigenous music was played with rattles, drums, flutes and conch-shell horns as part of religious celebrations. The Spanish introduced violins, guitars, harps, brass instruments, and woodwinds, which mostly replaced the native instruments. The European instruments were introduced to be used during Mass but were quickly adapted to secular events. Indigenous and mestizo peoples learned to play and make these instruments, often giving them modified shapes and tunings. In addition to instruments, the Spanish introduced the concept of musical groups, which, in the colonial period, generally consisted of two violins, a harp, and various guitars. This grouping gave rise to a number of folk musical styles in Mexico.

Mariachi groups today may have six to eight violins, one or two guitars, and several trumpets, and a guitar—all standard instruments—along with a "vihuela," which is a high-pitched, round-backed guitar that serves as the bass of the ensemble, and sometimes a Mexican folk harp to increase the baseline. These latter two instruments have European origins, but in their present form, they are strictly Mexican.

Mexican Piñatas

THE SALSA CULTURE INVADES AMERICA

The traditional Mexican celebration of birthday parties for children involving the breaking of the piñata or "cartoneria" (popular figurines made by craftsman utilizing cardboard, paper mache or newspapers) is one of the most anticipated activities awaiting families. The most popular figurines are now associated with Batman, Superman, Spider Man, Nemo, the Lion King, etc. The piñatas are usually filled with different sorts of candies that will be collected on the ground once a lucky child breaks it with a wooden stick. The piñata is hung on a rope overhead and maneuvered to and fro or from side to side by two individuals, oftentimes dropped from the top of a roof or from a tree (about ten to twenty feet apart) in order to challenge the children to look for it while they are blindfolded. The fun part comes when loud screams and yelling are heard to offer some form of direction as to the location of the piñata so that children can swing hard at the moving object. All participants are given a specific amount of time to try and hit the piñata, starting with the youngest to the oldest ones in the party. As it often occurs, the older children are the victors, the ones who finally break the piñata completely open with its newspaper material scattered all around, revealing the precious candy that is to be gathered at random by all the lucky participants. Hence, the triumphant kids are seen with bags of candies that they themselves collected while shoving others for them. The unlucky ones, who collect some or literally no candies, are usually taken care of by the promoters of the parties, who stack candies separately so that they can have candy to enjoy too.

Vendors selling the popular characters previously mentioned in Mexico have been routinely apprehended by federal authorities, who seize their illegal merchandize for violating international copyright laws. Though these vendors are not familiar with copyright laws, they claim that this has been going on for decades without problems. After all, Mexico has been exporting popular piñatas to the US for many years. All that the vendors have had to do is to render full cooperation enforced by "los federates" (federal officials) who forced their infamous under-the-table schemes known as "la mordida."

This Mexican traditional is now widespread throughout the US as hordes of Mexican and American families buy piñatas to celebrate birthdays, Christmas festivities and posadas, Fourth of July, New Year's Eve (giving way to the new year), Mexican independence or September 16, and Cinco de Mayo, etc. Hardly no one knows what a piñata is all about.

The Origins of Mexico and Its Builders

Centuries later, modem scholars offer us more in-depth studies into the vast continent of Mexico. William H. Prescott, perhaps the most famous historian of the Ancient Americans and the continent they inhabited long before the arrival of the Spanish conquistadors, shares the following perspective:

> Midway across the continent, somewhat nearer the Pacific than the Atlantic Ocean, at an elevation of nearly seven thousand five hundred feet, is the celebrated Valley of Mexico. It is of an oval form, about sixty-seven leagues in circumference, and is encompassed by a towering rampart of porphyritic rock, which nature seems to have provided, though ineffectually, to protect it from invasion. The soil, once carpeted with a beautiful verdure, and thickly sprinkled with stately trees, is often bare, and, in many places, white with the incrustation of salts, caused by the draining of the waters. Five lakes are spread over the Valley, occupying one tenth of its surface. On the opposite borders of the largest of these basins, much shrunk in its dimensions since the days of the Aztecs, stood the cities of Mexico and Tezcuco, the capitals of the two most potent and flourishing states of Anahuac, whose history, with that of the mysterious races that preceded them in the country, exhibits some of the nearest approaches to civilization to be met with anciently on the North American continent.

Of these races, the most conspicuous were the Toltecs. Advancing from a northerly direction but from what region is uncertain, they entered the territory of Anahuac,. probably before the close of the seventh century. The Toltecs were well instructed in agriculture, and many of the most useful mechanic arts; were nice workers of metals; invented the complex arrangement of time adopted by the Aztecs; and, in short, were the true fountains of the civilization which distinguished this part of the continent in latter times. They established their capital at Tula, north of the Mexican Valley, and the remains of extensive buildings were to be discerned there at the time of the Conquest.

The noble ruins of religious and other edifices still to be seen in various parts of New Spain, are referred to this people, whose name, Toltec, has passed into a synonym for architect. Their shadowy history reminds us of those native races, who preceded the ancient Egyptians in the march of civilization; fragments of whose monuments, as they are seen at this day, incorporated with the buildings of the Egyptians themselves, give to these latter the appearance of almost modem construction. After a period of four centuries, the Toltecs, who had extended their sway over the remotest borders of Anahuac having been greatly reduced, it is said, by famine, pestilence, and unsuccessful wars, disappeared from the land as silently and mysteriously as they had entered it.

After the lapse of another hundred years, a numerous and rude tribe, called the Chichemecs entered the deserted country from the regions of the far Northwest. They were speedily followed by other races of higher civilization, perhaps of the same family with the Toltecs, whose language they appear to have spoken. The most noted of these were the Aztecs or Mexicans, and the Acolhuans. The latter known in latter times by the name of Tezcucans, from their capital, Tezcuco, on the eastern border of the Mexican lake, were peculiarly fitted, by their comparatively mild religion and manners, for receiving the tincture of civilization which. could be derived from the Toltecs that still remained in the country. This, in turn, they communicated to the barbarous Chichemecs, a large portion of whom became amalgamated with the new settlers as one nation.

The Mexicans, with whom our history is principally concerned, came, also as we have seen, from the remote regions of the North, the populous hive of nations in the New World, as it has been in the Old They arrived on the borders of Anahuac, towards the beginning of the thirteenth century, sometime after the occupation of the land by the kindred races. For a long time they did not establish themselves in any parts of the Mexican Valley, enduring all the casualties and hardships of a migratory life. On one occasion, they were enslaved by a more powerful tribe but their ferocity soon made them formidable to their masters. After a series of wanderings and adventures, which need not shrink from comparison with the most extravagant legends of the heroic ages of antiquity, they at length halted on the southwestern borders of the principal lake, in the year 1325. They there beheld, perched on the stem of a prickly pear, which shot out from crevice of a rock that was washed by the waves, a royal eagle of extraordinary size and beauty, with a serpent in his talons, and his broad wings opened to the rising sun. They hailed the auspicious omen, announced by the oracle, as indicating the site of their future city, and laid its foundations by sinking piles into the shallows; for the low marshes were half buried under water. On these they erected their light fabrics of reeds and ruches; and sought a precarious subsistence from fishing, and from the wildfowl which the Waters, as well as from the cultivation of such simple vegetables as they could raise on their floating gardens. The place was called Tenochtitlan, in token of its miraculous origin, though only known to Europeans by its other name Mexico, derived from their war-god, Mexitli. The legend of its foundation is still further commemorated by the device of the eagle and the cactus, which form the arms of the modern Mexican republic. Such were the humble beginnings of the Venice of the Western World.

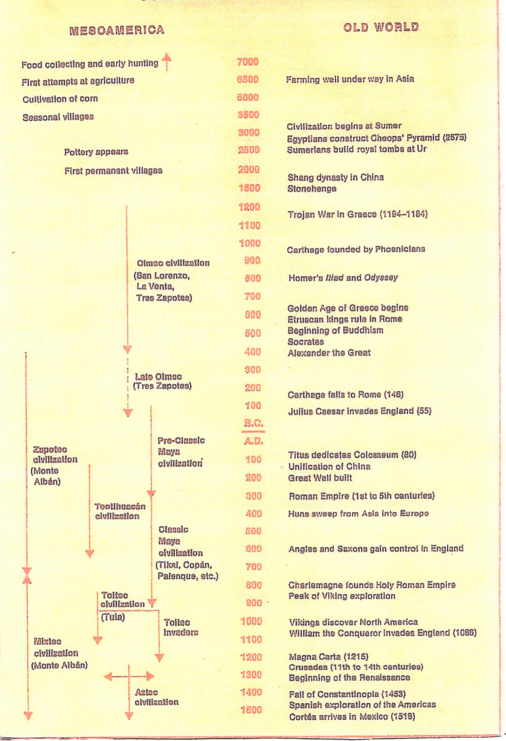

Source: Coe, Michael D., *America's First Civilization, Discovering the Olmec*, (The Smithsonian Library, American Heritage, 1968), 128–130.

One of the most famous relics of the Aztec civilization is this calendar, which represents the Mesoamerican concept of the time and the universe. A stone disk twelve feet in the diameter, its center is the sun carried across the sky by the fire serpents that encircles the rim. The ring of twenty symbols denotes the days of each month in the eighteen-month Aztec year. The signs around the sun depict the first four epochs of the earth. The Aztecs were in the fifth epoch when Mesoamerican civilization was utterly destroyed.

The Latino around the World

News articles report the Latino population is spreading and growing all over the world. Many have moved from the US to Europe, Africa, and Asia, spreading their Latino/American lifestyle through music, food, and dance.

The fastest growing groups in Italy, Switzerland, Spain, and Great Britain are the Latinos, and in Switzerland, the number of people who speak Spanish is almost as great as those who speak Italian. People in Switzerland up to this point speak French, German, and Italian respectively. Also, there are reports of many jobs available to Latinos in Europe.

Hispanics and Latinos are an ethnolinguistic group of Americans with genealogical origins in the countries of Latin America and Spain. More generally, it includes all persons in the United States who self-identify as Hispanic or Latino. Hispanic and Latinos are racially diverse, although predominately White or Mestizo. As a result of their racial diversity, Hispanics form an ethnicity sharing a language (Spanish) and cultural heritage, rather than a race. American Hispanics are predominately of Mexican, Puerto Rican, and Cuban ancestry.

Hispanics are the fastest growing ethnic group in the United States. As of 2012, Hispanics constitute 17 percent of the United States population or fifty-three million people. This figure includes thirty-eight million Hispanophobe Americans, making the US home to the largest community of Spanish speakers outside of Mexico, having surpassed Argentina, Colombia, and Spain within the last decade. Latinos overall are the second largest ethnic group in the United States after non-Hispanic whites (a group composed of dozens of subgroups like Hispanics and Latinos).

Hispanics have been in the territory of present-day United States continuously since the sixteenth-century founding of Saint Augustine, Florida, by the Spanish. Hispanics are the longest among US ethnic groups and second longest after Native Americans to inhabit what is today the United States.

Leaders Who Have Impacted the Mexican Mind and Spirit

There are so many leaders who have impacted the Mexican mind and spirit. The following list is by no means complete.

Benito Juarez

If we're looking for a true Lincoln, one who resembled the emancipator in spirit as well as in his political role, it is instructive to look at the life and career of Benito Juarez, who was born on March 21, 1806, in the Oaxaca, Mexico, village of San Pablo Gueletao. His parents, members of the Zapotec, prevalent in Oaxaca, were small farmers. Benito was not able to read, write, or speak Spanish. Yet he rose to become a priest; a lawyer; a city councilman in Oaxaca; a strong defender of Indian rights; governor of Oaxaca; director of his alma mater, the Institute of Science and Art; Mexican Minister of Justice; and participated in a new constitution for Mexico. In Guanajuato, in January 1857, he proclaimed himself president of Mexico.

Jose Vasconcelos

The intellectual Mexican philosopher, statesman, and national leader who has influenced the Mexican mind since the early 1900s. His philosophical contributions to the intellectual, social, economic, and political world are immense and well known in Mexican history.

Dr. Diana Natalicio

President of the University of Texas at El Paso (UTEP) since 1988, was named to the 2016 Time Magazine's "World's 100 Most Influential People." Thanks to her distinguished career in academia, the Education of Mexicans, Mexican Americans, the Latinos, the Hispanics, the Chicanos, and all other cultures in general, have benifitted from her powerful administrative abilities and God-given vision as to the educational goals and aspirations of these groups of people mainly situated in the Southern Border of the United States of America. UTEP is designated as a research/doctoral university now attended by a population of 23,000 up from her administrative start with 15,000 students. 80% are comprised of Mexican-Americans and 5% who commune to the campus fro Ciudad Juarez, Mexico. Dr. Natalicio was appointed by President George W. Bush to membership on the Advisory Commision on Educational Excellence for Hispanic Americans and by President Bill Clinton to The National Science Board. The president of Mexico presented her the *Orden Mexicana del Aguila Azteca,* the highest recognition bestowed on foreign nationals. The Carnegie Corporation of New York honored Dr. Natalicio with its prestigious *Academic Leadership Award* in recognition of her exceptional achievements during the transformation of UTEP into a national public research university. Additionally, Dr. Natalicio was inducted into the *Texas Women's Hall of Fame.* Dr. Natalicio's accomplishments are too lengthy to describe here and too numerous to record completely as of this time and place in history. A graduate of St. Louis University, Dr. Natalicio earned a master's degree in Portuguese and a doctorate in linguistics from the University of Texas at Austin.

Dr. Hector P. García

He was a Mexican revolution refugee, medical doctor to the barrios, decorated war veteran, civil rights activist, and presidential confidant. He fought to bring attention to the Mexican American civil rights movement.

There are many facts and stories about Dr. García. His life is well worth the research time. Basically, he fought against the discrimination of Mexican Americans while Dr. Martin Luther King was fighting for the African Americans.

Dr. García founded the American GI Forum, which supported Mexican Americans in the battles for their political and legal rights. During all of his fight for civil rights, he delivered babies and cured patients. Dr. García was appointed by President Johnson in 1967 as an ambassador (alternate) to the United Nations, and he gave a speech in Spanish. That was the first time an American had given a speech to the UN in a language other than English. He was the first Mexican American to serve on the United States Commission on Civil Rights.

President Ronald Reagan in 1984 awarded Dr. Hector P. García the Presidential Medal of Freedom. This is the highest civilian award given by the president of the United States, and Dr. García was the first Mexican American to receive the honor.

César Chávez

Chávez was the leader of the farmworkers of America. His firmness in defense of La Causa has much to be admired. Because of his efforts, farmworkers' lives have been improved substantially. His bold stance against farm owners who abused innocent, hardworking, and defenseless men and women, especially in California, still resonates in the Latino, Hispanic, and Mexican memory.

Corky Gonzalez

Corky Gonzalez' epic novel, *I Am Joaquin*, envelops the powerful Latino, Hispanic, and Mexican American spirits into one historical struggle to maintain their identity and dignity in pursuit of the American Dream. "I am Joaquin, lost in a world of confusion, caught up in the whirl of a gringo society, confused by the rules, scorned by attitudes, suppressed by manipulation, and destroyed by modern society. My fathers have lost the economic battle and won the struggle of cultural survival. And now I must choose between the paradox of victory of the spirit, despite physical hunger, or to exist in the grasp of American social neurosis, sterilization of the soul and a full stomach. Yes, I have come a long way to nowhere, unwillingly dragged by that monstrous, technical industrial giant called Progress and Anglo success . . . I look at myself. I watch my brothers. I shed tears of sorrow. I sow seeds of hate. I withdraw to the safety within the circle of life—I am Cuauhtémoc, proud and noble, leader of men, king of an empire civilized beyond the dreams of the gachupín Cortés, who also is the blood, the image of myself. I am the Maya prince. I am Chichimecas. I am the sword and flame of Cortéz the despot. And I am the eagle and serpent of the Aztec civilization.

Sonya Sotomayor

The nomination of Sonya Sotomayor (born in New York to parents from Puerto Rico) to become a Supreme Court justice of the United States attests to the growing influence of Hispanics in the judicial arena. And as Pedro Pierluisi, Puerto Rico's delegate to Congress said that it proves once again "that the American dream is available for all." It was generally agreed that her experience as an attorney, federal trial court judge and a Court of Appeals justice, along with her demonstrated intelligence, judicial experience, and independence made her eligible for her new position.

Raymond Tellez

Raymond Tellez was a true statesman, always a gentleman, and a true servant of the people. He was mayor of El Paso two times, county clerk four times. He served thirty years in the military and then as a civilian, acted as troubleshooter, and advisor to the federal government. He served as ambassador to Costa Rica under the Kennedy/Johnston administrations. That was a first for a Mexican American. At his death, Tellez (ninety plus years old) was designated as mayor emeritus of El Paso "in recognition of a pioneering Mexican American statesman with an unyielding commitment to his government, community and country."

Danny Olivas

Danny achieved his childhood dream of being an astronaut. John D. (Danny) Olivas was raised in El Paso and graduated from Burges High School. He received a degree in mechanical engineering from University of Texas at El Paso (UTEP) in 1989, a masters in mechanical engineering from the University of Houston, and a doctorate in mechanical engineering and materials science from Rice University. He is the first Hispanic in space, making his voyage in June 2007 and a second voyage in 2009. He and his space partner, Jim Reilly, installed a new segment of the International Space Station, and Danny repaired a damaged thermal blanket on the exterior of the shuttle.

Dennis J. Bixler-Márquez, Ph.D.

Dr. Bixler-Márquez is a native of Mexico City and had resided in the United States since childhood. He has lived most of his life is El Paso, Texas, from where he was drafted into the U.S. Army in 1966, serving a stint in Vietnam. He earned a B.A. degree in political science and Spanish and an M.E. in education (National Teacher Corp) from the Unversity of Texas at El Paso. He obtained an MA in Spanish and a doctorate in bilingual/multicultural education from Stanford University, where he became Associate Director of the Urban/Rural Leadership Development Program at the Center for Educational Research. He has taught at the University of Santa Clara and the University of Texas at El Paso. Dr. Bixler-Márquez is currently director of the Chicano Studies Research Program and the Center for Multicultural and International Education at the University of Texas at El Paso.

Dr. Bixler-Márquez is the author of several professional journal articles and monographs and co-editor of various tomes on topics such as *Chicano Speech in the Bilingual Classroom, Research Problems in U.S. Spanish, Long-Distance Multilingual Education in the Sierra Tarahumara, German-Spanish Bilingualism in Two Mennonite Communities.* He also serves on various national and international boards such as the National Consortium for Multicultural Sign Language Interpreting, the Mexio-U.S. Consortium for Academic Cooperation and the InterUniveristy Program for Latino Research.

Classic Mexican Songs

Cielito Lindo

Por la sierra morena vienen bajando, vienen bajando
Unos ojitos negros, Cielito Lindo, de contrabando

Coro: Ay, ay, ay, ay. Canta y no llores; porque cantando se alegran, Cielito Lindo, los corazones.

Pajaro que abandona su primer nido, su primer nido
Regresa y ya no en cuentra Cielito Lindo, el bien perdido.

Coro: Ay, ay, ay, ay. Canta y no llores; porque cantando se alegran, Cielito Lindo, los corazones. (Repite el coro).

Atotonilco

No te andes por las ramas uy, uy, uy, uy, uy, uy.
Camina trenecito que a Atotonilco voy.
Ya parece que en la estacion, da brinquitos mi corazon.
En ese Atotonilco de naranjos en flor,
Parecen las muchachas angelitos de Dios.
Son mas lindas que una cancion, de esas que son puro amor.
Atotonilco, tu cielo, tiene bellezas, tranquilas.
Como un rayito de luna, prendida en tu quietud.
Son tus mujeres preciosas cual florescitas hermosas,
Como un ramito de rosas, hermosas, uy, uy, uy, uy.

FÉLIX VALENZUELA

Alla en el Rancho Grande

Alla en el rancho grande, alla donde vivia; habia una
rancherita, que alegre me decia, que alegre me decia.

Te voy hacer tus calzones, como los usa el ranchero,
Te los comienzo de lana, te los acabo de cuero.

Nunca te fies de promesas, ni mucho menos de amores
Que si te dan calabazas, veras lo que son ardores.
(Se repite el coro despues de cada estrofa)

Pon muy atento el oido, cuando rechina la puerta
Hay muertos que hacen ruido, y son muy gordas sus penas.
Cuando te pidan cigarro, no des cigarro y cerillo
porque si das las dos cosas, te tantearan de zorillo.

La Cucaracha

La cucaracha, la cucaracha, ya no puede caminar,
porque no tiene porque le falta marihuana que fumar.
(Se repite)
La cucaracha, senores, siempre fue una mascotilla, y
a demas linda muchacha que llevaba Pancho Villa.
La cucaracha
Una vieja y un viejito, se cayeron en un pozo,
y la viejita decia, que viejito mas sabroso.
La cucaracha
Las mujeres de mi tierra, no saben ni dar un beso,
En cambio las Mexicanas, hasta estiran el pescuezo.
La cucaracha

Echale un Quinto al Piano

Echale un cinco al piano peseta de un jalon;
Y vengase mi prieta Pa en medio del salon.
Bailemos esta polka la rumba y el danzon; nomas se
me arrejunta y vera que vacilon.
Aflorje la cintura, no pierda su compas; y mueva la
cadera con mas velocidad,
Repeguese otro poco, no se haga para atras, ni se
haga tan ranchera y aprenda a vacilar.
Ay! Mamá, me aprieta este senor, Ay, Mamá, que
repegada estoy
Siento ya morirme de emocion.
Echale un cinco al piano y que siga el vacilon. (Se repite)

La Llorona

Todos me dicen el negro, Llorona, negro pero carinoso. (Se repite)
Yo soy como el chile verde Llorona, picante, pero, sabroso. (Se repite)
Ay, de mi Llorona, Llorona; de ayer y hoy. (Se repite)
Ayer era maravilla, Llorona, y ahora ni sombra soy. (Se repite)
Dicen que no tengo duelo, Llorona, porque no me ven llorar, (Se repite)
Hay muertos que no hacen ruido, Llorona, y es mas grande su penar.
Hay de mi Llorona, Llorona de azul celeste. (Se repite)
Y aunque la vida me cueste, Llorona, no dejare de quererte. (Se repite)
Si al cielo subir pudiera, Llorona, las estrellas te bajara. (Se repite)
La luna a tus pies pusiera, Llorona, con el sol te coronara. (Se repite)
Ay, de mi Llorona, Llorona de Negros ojos. (Se repite)
Ya con esta se despide, Llorona, tu negrito carinoso.

Mañanitas Tapatias

Que linda esta la mañana, en que vengo a saludarte;
venimos todos reunidos, con gusto a felicitarte.
Coro: Ya viene amanciendo Ya la luna se oculto.
Alevantate bien mio, mira que ya amanecio.

El dia en que tu naciste, nacieron todas las flores; y
en la pila del bautizo, cantaron los ruisenores. (Coro)
Diga si nos ha de abrir, pa no estamos esperando; no
somos tinajas de agua, para estarnos serenando. (Coro)

Serian las Dos

Serian las dos, serian las tres, serian las cuatro, cinco, seis de la manana,
cuando estaba con mi prieta platicando en su ventana.
Sale su mama de adentro tratandome de grosero, pero al punto yo le
digo soy Chupita, el parrandero.
Las muchachas de hoy en dia no saben comer tortillas; en cuantito que
se casan quieren pan con mantequilla.
Coro: Cuando tuve yo te tuve te mantuve y te di;
hoy no tengo ni te tengo ni mantego ni te doy. (Se repite)
Buscate otro que te tenga, te mantenga y te de,
Yo no tengo ni te tengo ni mante ni te doy.
Se repite:
Serian las dos, serian las tres, serian las cuatro, cinco, seis de la manana,
cuando estaba con mi prieta platicando en su ventana.
Sale su papa se adentro tirandome de balazos, y a la vuelta de su casa
nos dimos catorrazos. (Coro)

La Adelita

En lo alto de la abrupta serrania, acampado se encontraba un regimiento.
Y una moza que valiente lo seguia, locamente enamorada del sargento.
Pupular entre la tropa era Adelita, la mujer que el sargento idolatraba.
Porque a de mas de ser valiente era bonita, que hasta el mismo coronel
    la respetaba.
Coro: Y se oia, que decia, aquel que tanto la queria.
Que se Adelita se fuera con otro, la seguiria por tierra y por mar,
si por mar en un buque de guerra, si por tierra, en un tren militar.
Una noche en que la escolta regresaba, conduciendo entre sus filas al
    sargento;

Por la voz de una mujer que sollozaba, la plegaria se escucho en el campamento.
Y al oirla el sargento temeroso, de perder para siempre a su adorada;
Ocultando su emocion bajo el embozo, a su Amada le Canto de esta manera. (Se repite el coro)
Y despues que termino la cruel batalla, y la tropa regreso a su campamento
por las bajas que causara la metralla, muy diezmado regresaba el regimiento.
Recordando aquel sargento sus quereres, los soldados que volvian de la guerra.
Ofreciendoles su amor a las mujeres, entonaban este himno de la guerra.

La Valentina

Valentina, Valentina, yo te quisiera decir; que una
pasion me domina, y es la que hizo venir.
Dicen que por tus amores, la vida me han de quitar;
no le hace que sean muy diablos, yo tambien me se pelear.
Valentina, Valentina, rendido estoy a tus pies; si es
porque me ves borracho, manana ya no me ves.
Si es porque tomo tequila, manana tom Jerez; si me
han de matar manana, que me maten de una ves.

Classic Favorite Mexican Recipes

Menudo: The Breakfast of Champions

15–20 ibras de menudo
2 carteras de pata de puerco
2 latas de pozole
1 cabeza de ago
2 cebollas
1 paquete grande de chile colorado picante
sal al gusto, orégano, al gusto

Preparación:
Chile: Se cuece y se muele con 2 o 3 ajos y cebolla. Se cuela y se calienta hasta llegar a un hervor y se quita del fuego.

Menudo: Se limpia y se corta en cuadros chicos. Se lavan las patas. Se ponen el menudo y las patas a cocer con la cebolla y el ajo. Se cuecen por 3 o 4 horas o hasta que esté el menudo blandito. Se le quita la grasa y la espuma la primera vez que hierve. Cuando esté el menudo blandito se le agrega la sal y el chile preparado. Se cuecen el menudo y el pozole y la sal por lo menos 20 minutos.

Se sirve el menudo con cebolla cortada muy finita y con orégano al gusto, y pan francés.

Tamales de Chile Colorado con Carne

Tamales con masa preparada fuera de casa. Se pide la masa un poco seca para agregarle el caldo de la carne cocida, y más sal. Se prepara el chile colorado y se le agrega a la carne que anteriormente se ha desmenuzado.

Quando la masa este lista para poner en las hojas, se siguen las mismas instrucciones para los tamales con masa preparada en casa.

1 kilo de manteca o manteca vegetal
4 kilos de masa

Caldo de res o de pollo cocidos para los tamales, sal al gusto. Espauda, según la cantidad de masa que se utilice. Estas proporciones de carne a manteca se deberían usar en cualesquier caso. Chile colorado preparado de antemano, según las instrucciones en la sección de salsas, de este recetario. Tamales con masa preparada en casa.

1. Se cose la carne de res o de pollo con su propia sal, se desmenuza y se guarda el caldo.
2. Se prepara el chile colorado. Se le agrega a la carne que anteriormente se ha desmenuzado. La mezcla del chile con la carne debe estar jugosa, mas no debe chorrear al ponerse en la masa.
3. Se lavan las hojas en agua tibia, mas bien poco caliente, hasta quedar suaves y limpias sin barbas o basura.
4. Se prepara la masa en la siguiente manera: Se mezcla una porción (ya sea una libra o un kilo, conservando esta proporción) de grasa (ya sea de vegetal o de res) a cada cuatro porciónes (libras o kilos de masa). Se le agrega el caldo de la carne que se coció. Si no es suficiente él liquido para que amase bien la masa, se le puede agregar agua tibia hasta que este de una consistencia suave.
5. Se bate la masa con el caldo y sal hasta que levante la masa. Se le puede agregar una poca de espauda (muy poca) para que no de sabor amargo. Se sabe que la masa esta de Buena consistencia cuando una bolita muy pequeña de masa flota en una taza de caldo o agua tibia. Cuando este la masa lista, se ponen en las hojas.
6. Se pone una bolita de masa de aproximadamente 2 pulgadas de diámetro en una hoja de aproximadamente 4 x 8 pulgadas de ancho y largo. La masa se extiende sobre la hoja en una capa que cubra la hoja en un rectángulo de 3 x 5 pulgadas de ancho y largo.

7. Sobre la capa de masa se agrega una cucharada grande de chile con carne según el tamaño de la hoja. No debe chorrear el chile. Debe quedar una margen de cada lado de la hoja sin masa o chile para que no se deshagan en la cocida.
8. Se bobla la hoja en tercios, con la masa y el chile con carne por dentro. Si el tamal esta poco ancho, se amarra de arriba con un lazo pequeño hecho de hojas. Así el tamal no se deshace al cocerse.
9. Los tamales se ponen verticalmente en una olla honda con hojas de ma'z colocadas al fondo de la olla. Se le agrega suficiente agua a la olla para hacer vapor y cocer los tamales. Se cuecen al vapor por el tiempo necesario para que estén bien cocidos, según la cantidad de tamales que se hayan puesto en la olla. Es necesario calar los tamales algunas veces durante el tiempo que se cuecen para que no se quemen.
10. Cuando estén cocidos los tamales, se quita la olla de la lumbre y se deja enfriar. Después que se hayan enfriado, se sacan los tamales de la olla y se sirven. Si no se consumen inmediatamente, se refrigeran o se congelan hasta que se consuman.

Variaciones: Diferentes salsas de chile verde se pueden utilizar con el relleno. También se pueden rellenar los tamales de Frijóles, chile con queso, y otros ingredientes, según el gusto.

Caldo de Res the Traditional Mexican Way

1 kilo carne de res corte de cocido o de lomo
1 kilo de hueso de carrizo
½ cabeza de repollo
5 zanahorias largas cortadas en pedazos chicos
5 espigas de apio cortadas
1 cebolla en rebanadas
1 cabeza de ajo entero (despues se saca entero)
3 litros de agua, sal al gusto

Preparación de las verduras:
Se cose la carne junto con el carrizo por lo menos 2½ horas. Se le quita el gordo y la espuma que se forman al empezar a hervir. Se sala al gusto. La zanahoria y el apio se coceen por 15 minutos, tambien por separado. El repollo se cocee solo por 15 minutos. Despuéz que la carne de res esté blanda, se le agrega el repollo, el apio, y la zanahoria. Se coceen juntos por 30 minutos a fuego lento. Se cala el caldo para saber si tiene bastante sal y se retira.

Caldo de Res the Traditional Barrio Way

1 light weight 6" x 12" round aluminum container
1 bag of spare ribs (the square cut type)
6–10 small red potatoes (do not peel)
4–6 yellow whole corn (cut in half)
1 head of cabbage (cut into four equal parts)
½ bag of long carrots (peeled and cut into pieces)
2 pieces of squash (cut into pieces)
1 bag of cilantro

Preparation:
Fill half of an aluminum container with water and boil. Put the spare ribs into the boiling water and boil for at least 1½ to 2 hours. Put cut corn and carrots into container and boil for ½ an hour. Put the potatoes and continue boiling for ½ hour. At this point, the spare ribs, the corn, the potatoes, and the carrots have been boiling for at least 2½–3 hours. The final part includes the putting of the cabbage and pieces of cilantro (preferably without the stem) and boiling for another 15–20 minutes. Season with Lawry's Seasoned Salt according to taste. Simmer and serve with prepared Mexican rice.

Gorditas Mexicans

2 libras de masa de maíz
1 libra de carne molida

1 libra de queso
2 papas medianas
1 cucharada de espauda
1 lechuga picada
1 diente de ajo

Salsa de chile verde o rojo, al gusto, pimienta molida, al gusto, tomates picados, al gusto, cominos, al gusto, aceite, el necesario para freir las gorditas.

Preparación:
En un sarten con poco aceite, se cuece la carne y las papas poniendoles la sal, un ajo, y los cominos. Ya cosida la carne y las papas se separa el caldo y se guarda. Ya cocidas se muelen las papas con la carne y se guardan. Por separado, a la masa se le pone la sal, la espauda y poco comino y con el caldo reservado, se amasa. Cuando quede la masa suave se hacen las gorditas de 3 a 4 pulgadas de diámetro. Se fríen en aceite hasta que estén doradas. Después que estén fritas se abren y se rellenan de carne molida con papas que está preparada y se les agrega el queso y lechuga como adorno. Se sirven con tomate picado, chile verde o rojo, al gusto.

Variación: Para evitar demasiadas calorías no se fríen las gorditas en el aceite; la masa se amasa con agua y no con el caldo de la carne y papas y simplemente se cuece sobre la parrilla sin freírse.

Horchata de Arróz

1½ tazas de arróz blanco
8 tazas de agua
1½ tazas de azúcar, o al gusto
2 cucharitas de vainilla, o 2 rajas de canela
5 tazas de hielo (cubitos)
1 bote de leche evaporizada (grande)

Preparación:
Se remoja el arróz en agua durante la noche o de 8 a 12 horas. Se muele bien el arróz en la licuadora y se agrega agua para molerlo. Se cuela después que se licua. Se licua el arróz una vez mas con el azúcar y la vainilla agregándose la leche y el hielo.

Champurrado

1 bolsa de pinole
2–3 piloncillos
2 rajas de canela
1 tablilla de chocolate
1 bote de leche evaporada

Leche fresca, al punto que quieran de e spesor, pizca de sal.

Preparación:
Se pone el agua a hervir y se le agrega el piloncillo, la canela, el chocolate, la leche debote y la sal. Se disuelve el pinole en la leche fresca. Se cuela la mezcla y se le agrega al agua que está hirviendo. Se menea constantemente para que no se queme y se deja que hierva otra vez.

Variación: Con maza de maíz o Maseca.

Empanadas de Piña

Masa
7 tazas de harina
1 lata de 12 onzas de cerveza
1 libra de manteca

Preparación:
Se bate la manteca, se agrega la harina y se amasa usando la cerveza hasta que quede la masa como para tortillas. Se separa la masa

haciendo testales. Se extienden las testales y se pone la cantidad de relleno en el centro del círculo, se doblea por la mitad y se sella con presión en las orillas. Puede usarse un tenedor o el dedo para pegar las orillas. Se ponen las empanadas en una cazuela de hornear y se hornean por 30 a 35 minutos a 350°F grados.

Picadillo

1 Cebolla mediana, picada
1 libra de carne molida de res
¾ taza de jerez (opcional)
1 diente de ajo, picado finamente
¼ taza de pimiento rojo, picado
1 lata de 16 onzas de tomates en trozos
1 una taza de piña en cubos fresca o envasada
1 pizca pimiento rojo molido
¼ una taza de pasas
½ cucharadita de comino
½ cucharadita de orégano
1 pimiento verde picado, Sal, al gusto

Preparación:
En un sartén grande de fuego mediano, se dora la carne molida, la cebolla y el ajo hasta que la cebolla esté blanda, y la carne haya perdido su color rosado y el liquido que suelte la carne salga claro. Se escurre toda la grasa que se suelte. Se le agregan los demás ingredientes, excepto los pimientos. Se cuecen lentamente durante 5 minutos. Se le agrega los pimientos y se cuecen hasta que se clienten un poco. Se sirve con arróz y pan.

Pastel Tres Leches

Pastel
2 tazas de azúcar
8 huevos, separados

THE SALSA CULTURE INVADES AMERICA

1 cucharada de vainilla
2 tazas de harina
1 cucharada de espauda
½ taza de leche

Baño
2 yemas de huevo
2 latas de 12 onzas de leche evaporada
1 lata de 14 onzas de leche condensada
2 tazas de crema (mezcla de sour cream y whipping cream)
2 cucharadas de vainilla

Merengue
½ barra de mantequilla o margarina
1 queso crema chico
½ taza de azúcar pulverizada (o más, al gusto)
4 onzas de piña picada de bote sin el jugo
½ taza de nuez picada
½ cucharada de vainilla

Preparación: Se precaliente el horno a 350°F grados. Se engrasa y en harina un molde de pan de 9 x 13 pulgadas y 4 pulgadas de hondo.

El Pastel: Se bate juntos el azúcar y las yemas de huevo hasta que se haga una pasta amarilla. Se agregan la vainilla, harina, polvo de hornear, y leche mezclándose bien. Por separado se baten las claras de huevo a que queden duras. Se les agregan las claras a la masa cuidando no perder volumen. Se vierte la masa en el molde preparado y se hornea hasta que esté ligeramente café, como 30-40 minutos.

El Baño: Se licuan las yemas de huevo, las tres leches y la vainilla. Se le hacen agujeros desde la parte superior del pastel hasta el fondo y se vacía la mezcla sobre él para empaparlo estando el pastel caliente. Se deja enfriar en el mismo molde.

El Merengue: Se baten todos los ingredientes con una batidora y se vierte sobre el pastel cuando esté frío.

Capirotada

6 bollillos poco seco
4 piezas de piloncillo
1 queso fresco o panela
2 tazas de cacahuate tostado
3 rodajas de cáscara de naranja
5 rajas de canela
5 clavos de especie
1 taza de grageas
1 taza coco rallado
1 taza nuez picada
½ barra de margarina

Preparación:
Los bollillos se cortan en 3 a 4 pedazos a lo largo, se acomodan en una charola y se doran ligeramente en el horno. Después de dorados se les unta poca margarina. Mientras se dora el pan, en una cacerola honda se calienta el agua con el piloncillo, la canela y el clavo hasta que se disuelva bien el piloncillo.

En un recipiente grande que tenga una tapadera muy firme se acomoda una capa de pan dorado, con el lado con margarina hacia el fondo del recipiente.

Se rocía una capa de cacahuate sobre el pan. Sobre el cacahuate se acomodan rodajas de naranja y rajas de queso, el coco y nuez se roc'a sobre la capa. Sobre esto se forma otra capa de pan dorado y se alternan las capas hasta que se agoten los ingredientes. La capa final debe llevar rajas de queso, cubiertas con la gragea.

Cuando se hayan acomodado los ingredientes, se vacía el agua con piloncillo con cuidado sobre las capas de pan y queso, y se cuida que haya suficiente liquido al fondo del recipiente. Se vacía una cantidad de liquido suficiente para cubrir el pan hasta la última capa. Se tapa firmemente y se cuece a vapor con fuego lento por

40–50 minutos. Debe cocerse bien el cacahuate. Se puede servir la capirotada caliente o fr'a, al gusto.

Flan

1 cuarto de leche desgrasada
5 huevos
5 cucharaditas de sustituto de azúcar
1 cucharaditas de extracto de vainilla

Preparación: Se calienta la leche hasta que suelte vapor. Se baten huevos hasta que estén espumosos. Gradualmente se vacía la leche en los huevos y se agrega el sustituto de azúcar y la vainilla. Se vacía la mezcla en una cacerola sin engrasar y se pone la cacerola dentro de una olla para asar (como la que se usa para asar pavo). Se cubre la cacerola con papel de aluminio y se le agregan 2 pulgadas de agua a la olla para asar. Se hornea a 325°F grados por 60–75 minutos o hasta que el flan esté firme.

Tortillas de Harina

6 tazas de harina
1½ cucharaditas de espauda
2½ cucharaditas de sal
1 taza de manteca vegetal y agua tibia

Preparación: Se pone la harina, la sal y la espauda en una olla y se mezclan. Se le agrega la manteca y se desbarata con la mano mezclándose con la harina. Se le agrega el agua poco a poco hasta que la masa quede suave. Se hacen las testales y se palotean. Se cuecen en una plancha caliente

Pan Dulce

1 kilo de harina
1 taza de azúcar
6 huevos
1 taza de agua tibia
3 cucharadas de levadura
200 grams manteca
200 grams mantequilla

Preparación:
Se mezclan la harina y el azúcar. Se les agregan los huevos, la mantequilla, la manteca, y la levadura disuelta en una taza de agua tibia. Se amasa bien y se deja reposar hasta que se esponje. Se hacen las bolitas. Se ponen las bolitas, o conchas, en ena charola engrasada.

Adorno:
300 grams manteca
300 grams harina
300 grams azúcar

Se bate la manteca con la harina y azúcar hasta formar una pasta con que se adornan las conchas. Se hornean a 355°F grados por 30 minutos.

Ensaladas de Fruta con Yogurt

3 cucharadas de miel
3 cucharadas de jugo de limón
1 manzana, picada sin centro
1 naranja grande, pelada, cortada en rodajas
1 toronja grande, pelada y seccionada
1 plátano (banana), pelado y cortado en rodajes
1 litro de helado de yogurt con sabor a vainilla

Preparación:
En una olla grande se mezcla la miel con el jugo de limón. Se agregan las frutas y se revuelven. Se sirve con una bola de helado de yogurt encima. Se sirve con empanadas.

Ensalada Watergate

3 taza de Cool Whip
¼ taza de almendras en rajas
1 lata de 20 onzas de piña molida
1 caja pequeña de pudding instantáneo sabor a pistacho
½ paquete pequeño de bombones

Preparación:
No se cocina el pudding; simplemente se polvorea sobre la piña y se mezcla. Enseguida se agrega el Cool Whip y las almendras. Por fin se agregan los bombones. La mezcla debe tomar un color verde suave.

Banna Caribeña

1 plátano
½ taza crema dulce
¼ taza azúcar morena
3 bolitas de nieve vainilla
½ barra de matequilla

Preparación:
Se pela el plátano. Se corta por la mitad y luego en 4 partes. Se dora en la matequilla y se le agrega el azúcar. Se cuecen hasta que se haga el caramelo. Se agrega la crema y se mezcla. Se sirve con la nieve.

Calabacitas

1 libra de calabacitas
2 cucharadas cebolla picada

1 diente ago picado
2 cucharadas mantequilla o margarina o aceite
½ cucharadita sal
1 tomate chico picado
1 taza de queso rallado (opcional)
Preparación:
Se lavan las calabacitas y se les cortan ambas orillas. Se cortan en rodajas y se separan. En un sartén de 10 pulgadas a fuego lento. Se mezcla la mantequilla con la cebolla y el ajo hasta que estén tiernitos. Se agregan las clabacitas, el tomate y la sal. Se cubre y se cuece a fuego lento por 15 minutos meneando de vez en cuando hasta que estén firmes, sin recocerse.

Variación: Después de haberse cocido las calabacitas, se pueden cubrir con queso rallado, se tapan y se calientan hasta derretirse el queso. También se le puede agregar maíz de bote a las calabacitas.

Quesadillas

8 onzas de queso blanco, rallado
6 tortillas de harina, o tortillas de maíz
1 tomate pequeño, picado
4 cebollas verdes medianas, picadas
2 cucharadas de chile verde, picado,
cilantro fresco, picado

Preparación:
Sobre una mitad de cada tortilla se rocía ¼ taza de queso, tomate, chile y cilantro. Se dobla la tortilla con el relleno de queso por dentro. Se calienta cada tortilla sobre una parrilla hasta que el queso se derrita.

Gucamole

3 aguacates grandes y maduros
1 tomate asado
2 chiles jalapeños
1 taza de crema
1 cucharada cebolla picada, sal al gusto

Preparación:
Se muelen bien los aguacates con el machucador y se le agrega la crema. Se mezclan bien. El tomate y los chiles se pelan y se pican finamente y se le agregan al aguacate. Por último se agrega la cebolla y la sal. Se sirve con tostadas.

Salsa de Chile Chipotle

2 latas de 14½ onzas de tomate guisado con su jugo (stewed tomatoes)
3 dientes de ajo machucados
2 chiles chipotles en adobo enlatados
2 cucharaditas de aceite vegetal
1 lata de pasta de tomate (tomato paste) de 6 onzas
1 taza de agua
2 cubos de caldo consomé, arróz, al gusto, hojas de hierba buena para dar otro sabor (opcional)

Preparación:
En una licuadora, se licuan los tomates con su jugo, el ajo, y el chile chipotle hasta que se forme una mezcla espesa. En un sartén grande se calienta el aceite a fuego medio. Se fríe en el sartén la mezcla de tomate y chile. Se le agrega el agua a la pasta de tomate y los cubos de caldo hasta que todo este bien mezclado. Se cuece la mezcla hasta que empiece a hervir.

Chicharrones

1 tomate tostado
1 diente de ajo
1 manojo cebolla de rabo
1 lata de salsa de tomate, chile jalapeño, al gusto, sal, al gusto

Preparación:
Se licua el jalapeño tostado junto con las cebollitas, tomate, ajo y salsa de tomate. Se hierve la mezcla junto con los chicharrones y la sal hasta que estén blandos.

Enchiladas de Queso

2 tazas de chile colorado preparado o 2 latas de 8 onzas de salsa para enchiladas
12 tortillas de maíz
1 libra de queso cheddar o queso blanco, rallado cebolla mediana, picada, tomate, picado, al gusto, lechuga picada

Preparación:
Se calienta el horno a 400°F grados. Se calienta una taza de chile colorado o una lata de salsa para enchiladas en una cacerola hasta que empiece a hervir. Se pone la otra taza de chile colorado o de salsa en un recipiente hondo. Se remojan las tortillas en el chile colorado o salsa, una por una hasta que se ablanden. Se saca la tortilla y se rocía con el queso rallado y una pizca de cebolla. Se enrolla la tortilla y se coloca con las orillas hacia abajo en el recipiente hondo. Se cubren las enchiladas con el chile colorado o salsa restante, queso y cebolla. Se cubre el recipiente con papel aluminio o se hornea por 15 minutos. Se sirven con tomate y lechuga picados.

Mistaken E-Mail

A married couple decides to spend their vacations in the Carribean at the same hotel and beach where they celebrated their honeymoon 20 years before. However, the wife is not able to travel with her husband due to some problems at work but plans to meet up with him some days later.

Upon his arrival to the hotel the husband settles himself comfortably in his suite. To his surprise he notices a computer wit Internet access. He promptly decides to send an e-mail to his wife. But, he mistakenly presses the wrong key and enters the wrong word. Unaware of his mistake, he sends the e-mail to another address.

The e-mail is received by a widow who had just returned from her husband's funeral and upon reading the electronic correspondence faints and collapses instantly. Her son enters the room and discovers his mom on the floor unconscious.

Glancing at the bottom of the computer screen he notices the e-mail which reads:

My beloved wife, I have arrived well… Perhaps it may be of surprise to you to know that they have computers over here and one can send message messages to their loved ones. I have just arrived and it has been confirmed to me that all is in place in preparation for your arrival this coming Friday. I miss you very much and hope you have a pleasant and relaxing trip just like mine.

P.S. Bring minimal clothing; it is an inferno here, the heat is unbearable.

Bibliography and Recommended Reading

Anderson, Hans Christian (1845). The Little Match Girl, Wikipedia.

Atencio, Paulette. *Cuentos from Long Ago.* University of New Mexico Press: New Mexico, 1999.

Coe, Michael D. *America's First Civilization.* American Heritage, 1968.

Dennis J. Bixler-Márquez, Carlos F. Ortega, Rosalía Solórzano Torres, Lorenzo LaFarelle, "Latinos around the World," Chicano Studies, Survey and Analysis, Kendall/Hunt Publishign Company, 1997.

Diaz-Guerrero, R. *Psychology of the Mexican.* University of Texas Press, 1967.

Dinger, Adeline Short. *Folk Life and Folklore of the Mexican Border.* Hidalgo County Historical Museum, 1972.

García, Mario T. *Desert Immigrants.* Yale University Press, 1981.

González, Rafael Jesus. "Pachuco: The Birth of a Creole Language." *Arizona Quarterly* 23, no. 4 (Winter 1967).

Hoenig, Mark. "Curanderismo, A study from the Centro de la Familia de Utah." Utah: Salt Lake City, 1993.

Manza, John. "Drawing Race-Based Lines Is Problematic."

Mendoza-Grado, Victor and Richard J. Salvador. FAQ. soc.culture. mexican UCLA.EDU.70.

Morales, Fred. *El Segundo Barrio*. El Paso, TX: Juarez Historical Museum, 2001.

Prescott, William H. (1843). "The History of the Conquest of Mexico." http://xroads.virginia.edu.

Valdés, Guadalupe (1996). *Con Respeto*. Columbia University, 1996.

Wikipedia, the free encyclopaedia, provided information for: Medicinal Application of Indian Herbs, La Illrona, St. Valentine's Day, Honoring the Dead, Matachines, Cinco de Mayo Celebration, 16th of September, Halloween, Quinceañeras, Mariachis, Latino Around The World, Braceros.

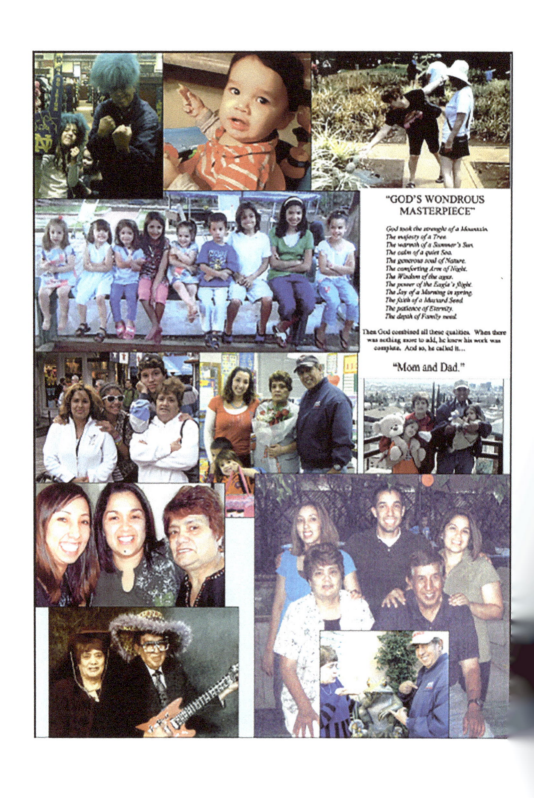

Trevor Hanes and Linda Heassler 2016

Sources

(On Gloria Castor's undergraduate research paper)

Alvarez, R. (2001). Los Re-Mexicanizados: Mexicanidad, Changing Identity and Long-term

Affiliation on the U.S.-Mexico border, Journal of the West, 22, 15-24.

Castor, Gloria. "Mexican-American Identity: Acculturation throughout generations." Undergrad paper, El Paso, TX: University of Texas at El Paso, 2002.

Sosa, M. (1999). Sense and Responsibility. Frontiers, 20, 97-105, (University of Texas at El Paso).

Mendoza, J. L (1994). On being a Mexican American, Phi Delta Kappan, 76(4) p. 293 -296).

Perez, W. Padilla, A.M. (2000). Cultural Orientation Across Three Generations of Hispanic Adolescents. Hispanic Journal of Behavioral Sciences, 22(3), 390-399.

Heyman, J.M. (2001). On U.S.-Mexico Border Culture. Journal of the West, 40(2), 50-51

"Cultural and Ecological Worldview Among Latino Schultz, P.W., Americans. Journal of Environmental Education, 2000, p. 1).

Knight, G.P, Cota, M.K., Bernal, ME. (1993). The Socialization of Cooperative, and Individualistic Preferences Among Mexican American Children: The Mediating Role of Ethnic Identity. Hispanic Journal of Behavioral Sciences, 15(3), 291-310.

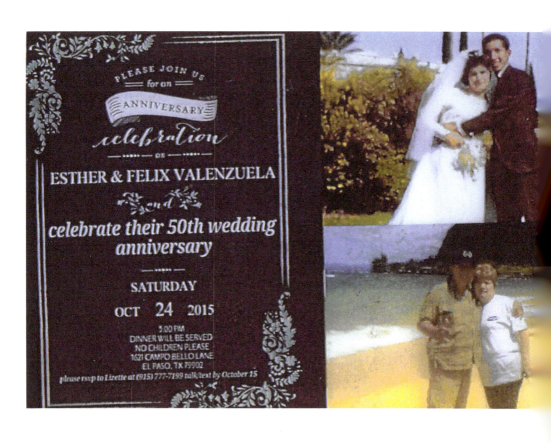

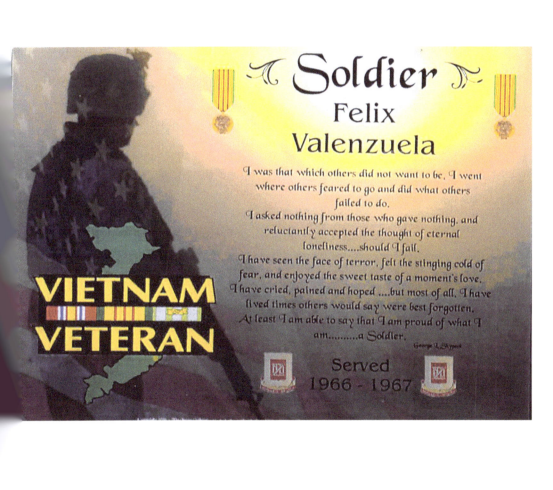

Credit to: "The official 2008 Visitors Guide, The Crossroads, Las Cruces, New Mexico."

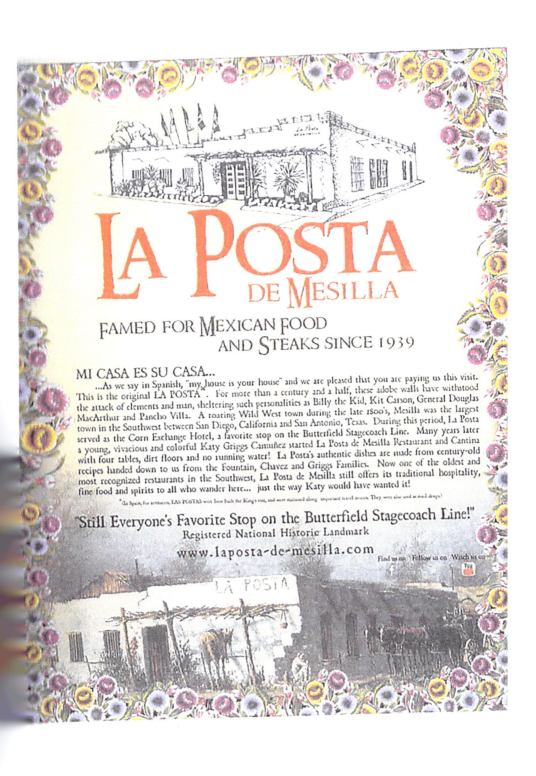

Jesus & Marlene de Zamora "WILSON ARCH"

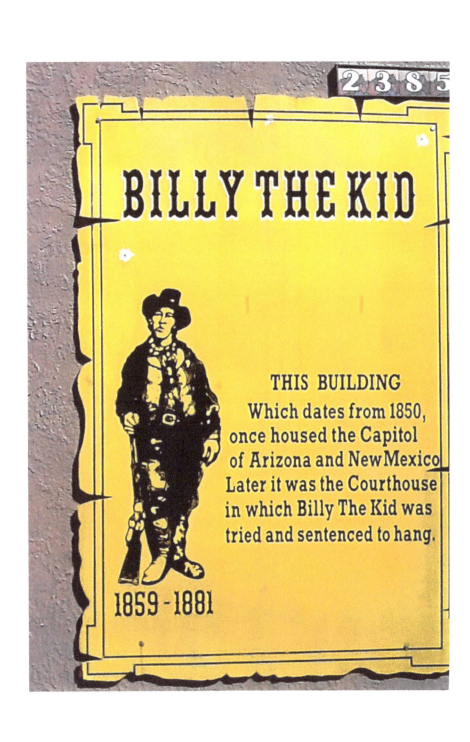

Former Chapel building of the historic 3rd Ward of The Church of Jesus Christ of Latter Days Saints, which once housed members under Guillermo Balderas Sr. the first Mexican Bishop in The Church of Jesus Christ of Latter-Day Saints.

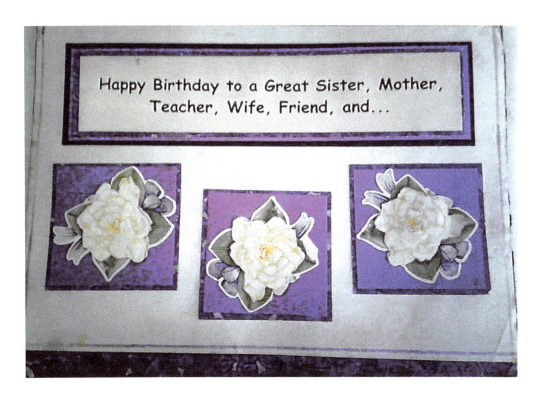

"THE BOWIE BAKERY" ...one of ex-U.S. President George W. Bush's favorite bakery in Texas.

"THE BOWIE BAKERY" …one of ex-U.S. President George W. Bush's favorite bakery in Texas.

"THE BOWIE BAKERY" …one of ex-U.S. President George W. Bush's favorite bakery in Texas.

"THE BOWIE BAKERY" …one of ex-U.S. President George W. Bush's favorite bakery in Texas.

"THE BOWIE BAKERY" …one of ex-U.S. President George W. Bush's favorite bakery in Texas.

About the Author

Felix Valenzuela was born in south El Paso in 1942 during World War II to Felix Ochoa and Maria Inez Carreon. He is the youngest of six siblings. His grandfather, Jesus Carreon, rode and fought with Mexico's infamous Gen. Pancho Villa during the Mexican Revolution in the early 1900s. Jesus Carreon and his brothers fled from Villa in fear, according to Felix, of repercussions for accumulating unauthorized material goods. They crossed the Rio Grande into the United States and landed safely in Clint, Texas, where they hid as farmworkers and general laborers until the revolution's end.

Felix's mother was born in Clint, but the family had moved to south El Paso by the time Felix was born. Felix says life in the barrio of South El Paso was the start of a long and arduous journey through the thresholds of American society for the Ochoa family. Felix attended Alamo Elementary when it was national policy to punish students engaged in speaking languages other than English. At Bowie and El Paso Technical High Schools, he excelled in sports and became El Paso Technical High School's first all-district and all-city baseball player and MVP for three years. Although he focused on the possibility of being drafted into a major league career in baseball, his life took a new direction. He elected to prepare for missionary work and was selected and called to serve among the first groups of missionaries in the country of Peru for the Church of Jesus Christ of Latter-Day Saints (LDS). Two and one half years later, he received an honorable release from service and returned to El Paso in 1965. He married Rosa Esther Pinon and after only two months of marriage, he was drafted into the United States Army and served in the Vietnam conflict. He was assigned to Long Binh (adjacent to Bien Hoa Airport). When the Communist North Vietnamese infiltrated the American perimeter and blew up the US Army's ammunition dump, the largest in Vietnam, Felix ran for cover and fell into a deep ditch full of rocks. He received a serious back injury which put an end to his baseball career. When he returned to the States, he attended the University of Texas at El Paso, eventually became a placement officer within the UTEP system, and then opened up his own construction company, followed by a beauty salon and a video store. After Felix and Esther had operated this business combination for ten years, they decided to move to Salt Lake City, Utah. Felix became state director for the Migrant and Seasonal Farmworkers (1992–1995) under the direction of the Utah Board of Education. The weather was extremely cold and Felix and Esther missed El Paso. About that time, they were involved in three different car accidents and decided to come home.

Felix reopened his construction business in El Paso and took an interest in city government. He served six years on the El Paso Parks and Recreation Advisory Board during the mayoral terms of Ramirez, Caballero, and Cook. In 2010, he was elected to the Project Bravo board of directors (Northeast, District 4) and served three years. He also put his time and effort into the Machela O'Oba International Indigenous Foundation, along with being called to serve his church as president of the Transmountain Branch (El Paso, Texas Mt. Franklin Stake.)

Felix and Esther have three children. Felix Jr. got his law degree from Yale University, worked for the US District Court in El Paso and now has his own law firm in the Wells Fargo Bank building in downtown El Paso. He was selected on May 4, 2013, as "Outstanding Young Lawyer by the Young Lawyers Association" for 2012-2013 and on January 22, 2016, the Mexican-American Bar Association of El Paso selected him as "Outstanding Lawyer" for 2015-2016. Lizette is a graduate of Brigham Young University. She has worked for the Texas Child Protective Services and Mental Health and Mental Retardation. She is a licensed professional counselor and works with the Emergence Health Network in El Paso. Linda is returning from Hawaii where she lived with her husband who was an U.S. Army Major. She is working toward a degree in education and English literature.

Esther retired from cosmetology when she contracted cancer. During her fight against cancer, she attended the University of Texas at El Paso and was the only grandmother to graduate in the class of 2002. She is a second grade bilingual teacher in the El Paso Independent School District. Not only did she win her battle against cancer, but in 2009, she was nominated for Teacher of the Year. Esther retired in 2015 and is now a tutor in the El Paso Independent School District.

Felix spent many years on this book collecting information about the salsa culture for his children, grandchildren, future generations, and as it has turned out, for his friends. Everyone has been eagerly awaiting this book, and we are sure no one will be disappointed.

CPSIA information can be obtained
at www.ICGtesting.com
Printed in the USA
LVHW07s1712250718
584773LV00041B/246/P